Colin Skinner was born in Norfolk in 1955. He moved to London to study aged 18 and then to Brighton aged 21.

In 1978, aged 23, Colin became a freelance sound recordist for BBC TV news and current affairs. In 1982 he moved to London and working for Diverse Production, a new independent production company set-up and contracted to supply the recently established Channel 4 with current affairs programming. In 1983 he moved to camerawork and by 1987 was a freelance lighting cameraman, working on primetime factual TV shows such as Channel 4's *The Media Show*, the BBC's *Horizon* and many more influential and popular programmes.

Brought up with home cooking, Colin learnt and enjoyed cooking for family and friends, and developed a love for varied cuisines experienced at home and abroad.

COLIN SKINNER

MY LOCKDOWN COOKBOOK

AUSTIN MACAULEY PUBLISHERS™

LONDON • CAMBRIDGE • NEW YORK • SHARJAH

A CIP catalogue record for this title is available from the British Library.

ISBN 9781398494817 (Paperback)
ISBN 9781398494824 (ePub e-book)

www.austinmacauley.com

First Published 2023
Austin Macauley Publishers Ltd
1 Canada Square
Canary Wharf
London
E14 5AA

I dedicate this book to my wonderful friend Mike, who found it in himself to read all the way through, correcting my poor spelling and grammar and helping to re-arrange it in a better way.

I want to thank my lovely wife Juliet for helping me perfect these dishes and being patient as I photographed our supper! Thanks too to my girls for years of encouragement and their demands for recipes. Thanks also goes to my bridge boys, with whom I have enjoyed decades of fine home-cooked food, lively conversation and some great cards.

Contents

An Introduction

I am neither a writer nor a chef! I spent my life, and it was a privileged life, as a cameraman filming documentaries for British TV. I have been so lucky to travel widely and to experience so many of the world's cuisines, and it was that, and my love of food, that encouraged me to learn to cook. It has taken many years and quite a few rather odd dishes for me to become a decent home cook. I have written this book partly from the encouragement of people around me and partly because it's one of those things so many people say they cannot do! I say: they can, if I can!

Eating home-cooked food is not only a pleasure, it's also a benefit to our health. Cooking it, too, can become a great distraction, especially after (or during a break in) a day's work when relaxation and distraction are what is most required. When I am cooking, I find myself experiencing, in some ways, that mindfulness that is so good for our mental well-being. Often the radio is keeping me company and stopping those little 'noises off' from distracting me from the task. So, taken in the right way, cooking can be good not just for the body but the mind too. It's a real pleasure once that *fear of failure* has been left behind.

Celebrity chefs, *Master Chef* and *Bake Off* are great entertainment: in lockdown, they helped entertain us for many hours. The cooks on those programmes, however, tend to produce food that can seem too good to eat, often looking like a dish you would spend a fortune on at an expensive restaurant. For many people, this actually puts them off from learning better culinary skills. They think this high quality is what is expected and are quite reasonably put off before they get started. They cannot help but notice, too, the array of tools and machinery that seem to be needed. Yes, of course it's great to be able to cook and serve a pretty plate of delicious food. But cooking for your family and friends is not and need not ever be anything like these shows.

Food is essential for life, and so it makes sense for it to be an enjoyable and satisfying part of most days, not a chore. The recipes in this book are meant to be for everyday food for everyday people. Yes, some take longer than others, some are indulgent, and some are quick, but all are possible; with a little patience and with practice you can become a great home cook. All the ingredients here are available online and often quite locally too.

Scientists, biochemists, dietitians and many more experts in the field of food have so much to say about dos and don'ts. I believe it's quite simple. Fruit and veg and all things fresh and unadulterated are good. Nuts and seeds are a must. Meat and fish that have not been filled with antibiotics, growth hormones and other chemicals are good too, in moderation. (The mere idea of a 24-ounce steak truly shocks me.) Having said that, let's give ourselves a break every so often and buy a takeaway or a fast food meal. While we are at it, some of those pastes and sauces in bags and jars are not that brilliant, but used once a fortnight – or even once a week – in a shared meal they aren't going to do too much damage. It's just not possible to make everything from scratch all the time; in any case, hard and fast rules put me and most others off. Eating between meals is to be avoided, as it's the way many of us put on weight; but the homemade cakes and tarts and puddings have to be eaten, don't they?!

Cook an amount that is enough for those eating it. If there is some left over, do not always finish it: enough is enough, put it into a pot and pop it in the freezer for another day. Being 'full' after every meal is not good. You will slowly stretch that tummy and need more to feel satisfied. That saying 'everything in moderation' is truly appropriate here. Try to have no meat two or three days a week – red meat twice a week is plenty and some might say once a week is enough – and try to eat fish at least once every week. The meat or fish on your plate should not be the biggest part of your meal, that's a mistake: it should normally be no more than one quarter. So a typical meal might be the chipotle pork chops (page 108) – 4 to 5 ounces for a chop is big enough – plus a portion of potato wedges, coleslaw and tomato salad. It's a balanced meal. Try to habitually eat fruit or nuts after lunch and supper every day, maybe chopped into a bowl of kefir or yoghurt, or occasionally an indulgent spoon or two of clotted cream. But a selection of fruit daily is a very good habit to get into. Doing this, or trying to most of the time, should make your tummy happy and you feel good too. A happy tummy really is a good start to health, along with some regular exercise.

I have always put food on or near the top of life's pleasures. Cooking it can be very satisfying, too. But being sure to have enough time is important: so many people do not want to cook, and often it's just confidence and time that get in the way. Choose a dish that you can cook comfortably given the time you can devote or have available. Never try to make any winter stew, casserole, tagine, curry and so on without having lots of time to let it bubble away and keep an eye on it so it does not stick and burn. You do not need to be stirring or doing anything for quite useful periods of time, however; time for another half-hour of work or to help the kids with their homework! Braised chicken needs a minimum of 80–90 minutes to soften so the meat falls from the bone, whereas stewing steak or braising steak needs over two hours to lose that chewy nature. Fish, however – if you like it – is almost impossible to under-cook, as we love sashimi. Once it's cooked too long, though, it will fall apart and quickly turn into a disaster. Most fish portions are well cooked in less than 10 minutes in a pan or, as with the Japanese Baked Salmon (page 56) that cooks in the oven, 15 minutes is quite enough. Cook it more, and it gets tougher and then tougher still.

No recipe I have ever read or attempted has ever stayed the same. Over the months and years, I stopped reading the list of ingredients and the weight or quantity, preferring to 'do it my way' – a way that preferably makes it simpler and quicker to prepare, whilst adding to the pleasure and suitability for our particular home tastes.

With so many of the dishes I cook regularly I just grab a handful, or tip a bit in! It's a way with food that you too will develop, given time! How much time? Well, I am now 66, and a lot of things I have made for a while just happen that way, but your guess is often just as good as mine. When you have got used to the way flavours work – a tin of tomatoes in a Bolognese sauce works as well with 300g as with 400g of good minced beef, but if you don't think it's quite enough, add a squeeze or two of tomato paste – then you have started to feel confident and that's all it is.

Cooking certainly is not rocket science, but then, when confronted by a complex-sounding recipe in a cookbook, too many of us do not even make a start. Making a mess of a recipe is not a big deal: it's the learning process. And this is why I have put this book together. I used to think many types of food were beyond my ability to cook well, but slowly I realised that's not true! I could probably follow some of those French recipes that literally take all day and sometimes into the next day too, but that's just not home cooking to me. There are still lots of French dishes that can be cooked in a few of hours, and that's long enough for me. Learning to be a sushi chef in Japan takes many years and learning true French gastronomy decades, and that is not what home cooking should ever be about.

So it's learning about ingredients and how to understand the vagaries of differing aspects of them that's a key to understanding how to be a decent home cook. Herbs are a fine example. A handful of thyme from the garden is many times stronger than a handful of parsley, while homegrown basil is twice as pungent and flavoursome as a bag bought from the supermarket.

Freshness is key to so many foods. Cavolo nero bought straight from the local farm shop can be cooked twice as quickly as the bag from the supermarket. Tomatoes, when fresh and not shipped from another part of the world, have so much more flavour that they are almost a different fruit altogether (yes, a fruit!).

Chillies are not possible for everyone. Small, red ones are hot, yes, but chillies vary and vary in size. The white or pale strip inside and the seeds that are attached to it are the really hot parts. So how can anyone be able to regulate with any accuracy the 'heat' of any dish? In my experience one has to resort to bought dried chilli! It's a shame chillies cannot be sold with a heat rating of say 1 to 5 (or better probably 1 to 10): that would really help. I still use fresh, though, as they do have a flavour as well as that heat!

So the way in which any dish can vary has so many different aspects that it's hard to be able to confidently say how long you should cook or how much of an ingredient you should use, or anything really. Which is why that 'confidence' that will develop given time is such an important element in being able to enjoy cooking and eating at home.

A pressure cooker can really help some things, like 'Mum's beef stew' (page 95), which I have never tried to make without one. A pestle and mortar plus a spice grinder are pretty essential for almost all curries. My homemade Thai-style paste (page 20) is whizzed up in a 'bullet' blender, as it's made in bulk and stored in portions. A good-sized casserole dish with a well-fitting lid can be regularly used for all those winter stews, braised chicken, tagines and many lovely dishes. Some of these could be cooked in a pot on the hob, but if you want to be able to leave it for a while, the dish may reduce and stick to the base of a pot, whereas a casserole dish will generally not do so at anything like the same rate, providing a tight-fitting lid is included. A small electric hand whisk is a very useful tool in all those dishes where beating eggs or cream is essential; doing it by hand is arm-aching and time-consuming.

The important thing is that if I can cook these dishes, so can you! There is not that much skill involved – yes, using sharp knives and chopping to various sizes can take practice, and there are a few things to always remember:

- Beef can be eaten from raw to browned all the way through, but most meats have to be cooked so as not to make you feel pretty sick.

- Chicken often contains *E.coli* and must be cooked thoroughly, and you must constantly wash your hands, knives and boards – but do not overcook chicken, as it will dry out.

- Cheap beef is tough as old boots unless cooked for quite some time, as in stews and pies in Europe or curries from the far east.

- Be careful with fish, especially mussels and other crustaceans, but whole fish can be eaten raw as in sashimi, so no worry about under cooking for your health, fresh fish when cooked just so, is a truly tasty and enjoyable thing.

Don't forget that today in the 21st century we have search engines that can answer any simple question about food in mere seconds, so always use these if in any doubt.

So here are some ideas. They are all quicker to prepare than the originals. I hope you enjoy trying some of them. There is something here for everyone.

Recipes from the Far East

I have been a huge curry lover for many years. I wish I had visited India more and eaten the real thing, but I was limited to one holiday in Kerala and stop-offs in Bombay and Delhi. South Indian food was as lovely as expected: coconut and fresh leaves, lots of fish, and veg I had never seen, heard of or eaten before. Fast food at the airport and street food outside was nothing in any way like any curry I had before: just those tastes showed the promise of much more. Sri Lanka, in my world, is heaven! Amazing food through the day with lovely cool beer, beaches out of a picture book with warm waters that still refresh, history, culture, verdant mountainous interiors and so much more. My first visit was in 1985, staying at The Villa, a wonderful colonial Dutch haven in the palms behind Bentota beach.

Before this, curry for me was mild, medium or hot, with a choice of meats or fish, veg or dhal on the side, but lacking delicacy or freshness. It was popular and quickly became a staple meal out or takeaway for many of us. Not knowing any better, I for one somehow assumed this was indeed Indian food. Time persuaded me otherwise. So Sri Lanka in 1985 was the beginning for me of a love of all things curry. I had no idea a samosa could be so enjoyable, a bel-puri too, a dhosa and even a sublime version of a Scotch egg. Every lunch and every supper was a memorable experience: bursting with flavours new to me, combinations of spices so fresh it was overwhelming. I ate like a king! I tried everything; I filled myself to bursting at times just to know what a 'breakfast hopper' was or to savour a pile of spiced prawns, fresh from the sea only hours before, that were nearer the size of a lobster than prawns I had seen previously. Endless dips, sambals and chutneys on the side were little grenades of flavour, enjoyed like every other mouthful. It is no wonder that this marvellous little hotel became renowned the world over: not just for its architecture or its perfect location on a perfect beach but also for its amazing chefs.

Indian food has, for many years – decades, in fact – been the British favourite. A night out followed by a flaming vindaloo was Friday night. Fish and chips or a kebab played second fiddle to the ubiquitous curry. Slowly, we came to realise that this style of cooking was more or less invented for us by the Indians. All the way back to the era of empire when some smart chef invented kedgeree for his masters, the cuisine was moulded to our tastes. Finally, today, we have many 'Indian' restaurants serving what some say gets nearer to true Indian cuisine.

For me, Meera Sohda's many wonderful books, describing her take on an Indian family living in an English town and cooking their food with what they could buy or grow, have been the very best lesson in 'Indian cooking'. I have cooked so many of her recipes and messed about with them to make them suit my own taste and sometimes to speed up the process. Her biryani is fantastic.

I always thought that a properly cooked biryani would be a true pleasure. However, most restaurants cannot do this dish justice as it takes so many hours of preparation, and it is truly best just when it's ready to serve. I bought a clay pot the right size and shape to make her version for four, and it is every bit as good as I hoped, if not better. Explore Meera's books – I still do, and I love them, to the extent that every new recipe is quite an exciting thing, even now!

To make a curry, almost any curry, a pestle and mortar and a spice grinder/blender are pretty essential to make the process bearable. Once you have these you can set out to cook and learn so many differing curries. Everything – almost, anyway – is available online or on your local high street. Be brave, and once you learn the basics you can make your own versions of many great dishes.

Most evening meals I make take no more than an hour, occasionally 90 minutes. That does not mean you are busy every moment of the hour; no, you will have time to help with the homework or other stuff. I feel it's so important that anyone can cook a tasty, healthy and enjoyable supper in about an hour. Some can be quicker, especially when you have a Thai paste ready-made in storage, so you can make a curry with rice and veg in 30 minutes. On the other side of that coin, there are some dishes that need to be started after breakfast that can be quick later or take some time through the day! The lamb biryani (page 38) or the Vietnamese beef rib (page 68), for instance: made for guests over a weekend, maybe?

Nearly all curries freeze very well, often actually benefiting from this. So although these can be a bit time-consuming, make plenty so you can freeze portions. (Cauliflower does not survive freezing at all well!)

Asian Curry Pastes and Powders

These shop-bought pastes are so good that every attempt I have made to cook anything like it has never been anywhere near as good or even good enough. They are quite easy, too. They are, in fact, one of our favourites: great on those days when I feel lazy or on 'that can't be bothered' day, when a gin and tonic in the garden seems perfect.

Basically, the smaller bags are for two persons, and the bigger ones are suitable for over a kilo of meat, which will feed quite a few people indeed. Like all good curries, they freeze very well too.

So, take one of the bigger bags and use about a third to a quarter of the paste. Put it in a saucepan and add chicken or beef for two. Stir this gently on a low heat. Slowly but surely, the meat looks cooked on the outside. Now we have two different ways to go. First, if it's chicken, add equal quantities of coconut milk and water to just a bit more than cover, chop one good size sweet potato and add to the pot and add a tablespoon of desiccated coconut. Now simmer for 40–45 minutes: at the end, it should be reduced to a thick gravy and the sweet potato softened.

If it's beef, simmer for one hour with the equal quantities of water and coconut milk and desiccated coconut. Then, add the sweet potato and simmer for another 40–45 minutes. This should also produce a nice thick gravy and softened meat and potato. If not, simmer till it is! That's it for both.

Being total Sri Lanka fans, my wife and I discovered some time back that the dishes served in some of our favourite restaurants can be bought online and enjoyed at home. The Villa restaurant is renowned for its Black Pork Curry and this can be almost reproduced with the packets of KOLUU curry mixes. There is quite a variety from this brand: Beef pepper, Red Chicken, Fish curry and others. Making them is quite easy. The instructions are on the pack and they are truly tasty – a touch hot, and so reminiscent of the country. I recommend them highly. The only quibble I have is cooking time: the beef certainly needs longer to cook than the instructions, and I prefer the result when coconut milk is substituted for half the water, but it's personal.

My Homemade Thai Curry Paste

Make this in a big batch, enough to fill your bullet to the brim. Then carefully fill lots of small pots that can be put in the freezer and used when you want it. I have square 0.15 litre pots, and that's perfect for a curry for two. They are really effective at keeping it fresh and fragrant.

1 hour

250g of fresh turmeric

250g lemon grass

250g fresh ginger (galangal is more authentic, but it's so tough it's hard to blend)

250g of shallots

1 garlic bulb

12+ lime leaves with the stalks removed

Juice and zest of 1 lime

1 tablespoons of fish sauce

4–6 tablespoons of peanut oil

2 teaspoons of shrimp paste (a jar that has oil in it too – not Belacan)

1 large bunch of fresh coriander, thoroughly washed

1 tablespoon of coconut sugar

Quite a few turns of the salt grinder

So, blend it well. Do not run the bullet for more than 90 seconds at a time! Leave for a few minutes and keep repeating till you have a smooth paste. If the bullet starts to get hot, pause for longer! You maybe have to add more oil; if so, add a little at a time. This takes 20–25 minutes. Be patient, as it's worth it!

You should end up with quite a few little frozen boxes to enjoy later, and it should be truly blended and smooth. Recognise, however, that homemade smooth will never be as smooth as bought pastes. The makers' machinery is more powerful than the domestic counterparts and blends whatever it's asked to.

To cook: defrost, then, on a low heat, add the paste to a small saucepan and add a couple of teaspoons of coconut milk. Stir and fry gently. When it's fragrant, add diced chicken or some prawns or your choice of veg. Cook till the meat or fish is beginning to change colour and then add no more than a quarter of a can of coconut milk. Simmer this for 15–20 minutes – and it's done. Look for the oil to start separating out: the paste and the chicken has quite a bit of oil, and this starts rising to the top when it's done. My own paste is still one of my favourites. There is more turmeric and ginger than would be in most 'authentic' pastes, but it this that makes my tummy feel like it's smiling after a chicken or prawn curry with sticky rice, kimchi, pickles and a bit of something green.

Homemade Teryaki Sauce

Having bought the Kikkoman brand of this sauce for many years, it was quite disconcerting to see it vanish from the shelves during the pandemic and only pop up occasionally in smaller bottles. So I decided to do a bit of browsing and, as ever with a bit of adjusting to my own tastes, this is what I came up with.

½ a cup of best Japanese soy sauce

A quarter cup of brown or coconut sugar

A large chunk of grated ginger, squeezed so all the liquid is extracted

A tbsp of honey

2 tsp sesame oil

3 tbsp mirin sauce

Just put all this lot in a small saucepan and bring to the boil, then simmer for 10 minutes or so. If you are doing a BBQ or simply want a thicker cause to glaze, then add a thickener like arrowroot or cornflour so that the sauce thickens.

My way with this sauce is like so many marinades: just popped into a plastic freezer bag and massaged every so often till you are ready to cook. It works particularly well with chicken or beef, not to mention salmon and many other fish.

Once you have cooked the meat or fish in a hot pan (splatters quite a bit!), you should remove it to a serving plate and then de-glaze the pan with a little more sauce. Heat it all till it's bubbly, then pour over the cooked meat or fish.

Serve with rice and Japanese cucumber salad and/or Japanese spinach.

Bombay Potatoes

If you fancy a curry without rice for any reason, there are plenty of recipes for potato. This is my favourite: it's pretty foolproof and reasonably quick.

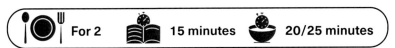 For 2   15 minutes   20/25 minutes

Partially boiled potatoes (not soft, still firm)

A small piece of ginger

A few garlic cloves

1 shallot

1 mild red chilli

1 tsp mustard seeds

1 tsp cumin seeds

1½ tsp coriander seeds

1 tsp turmeric

1 tsp garam masala

2 good size tomatoes

Chopped fresh coriander

Salt and pepper

Finely chop the ginger, shallot, and garlic. Fry gently, add the spices and stir, adding a little oil to be sure it's not too dry and does not stick. When it's all mixed and fragrant, chop the partly cooked potatoes and add them. Continue to fry gently, till the potatoes are soft and cooked. Turn regularly – and carefully, as you do not want the potatoes to break up. When you feel the potatoes are cooked, add the chopped tomatoes and finely chopped chilli, and turn them well into the potatoes. When it's all hot, turn into a serving bowl and sprinkle the fresh coriander over.

A Simple Chicken Curry

The following recipe is my regular homemade chicken curry. It allows you to get the feel of the herbs and spices that go into a curry, rather than just using 'curry powder'. From this simple start you will be able to add, subtract or whatever to turn it into your own chicken curry.

For 2   20 minutes   40 minutes

2 large or 3 medium boneless chicken thighs

3/4 tsp cumin seeds

3/4 tsp coriander seeds

1/3 tsp fennel seeds

3–4 cloves

1 good size shallot

3–4 garlic cloves

1 large chilli, de-seeded

1 thumb sized piece of ginger

1 thumb size piece of turmeric

3–4 tbsp oil (I use olive oil, peanut oil or coconut oil)

Ground pepper and salt

2 tbsp coconut milk

Toast the seeds till they begin to smoke, then finely grind to a powder. Blend the fresh stuff till it's a purée.

In a medium-size saucepan, heat a little coconut oil and pour in the purée and the ground seeds, mix well and fry gently for quite a few minutes till the oil begins to separate and the fragrance is released. Add the chicken meat roughly chopped into chunks and gently stir and fry for a good 10 minutes. Grind in some black pepper and salt, then add water to cover. Simmer away for 20-30 minutes till it's reduced, then add the coconut milk. Simmer till the gravy is no longer watery at all – not thick either, but somewhere in between.

Serve with 'My Dhal' (page 30) and spinach wilted into it, and rice or naan.

Twice Cooked Asian Pork Belly

I love pork belly! Like most of the cheaper cuts of meat, it needs time to bring out the flavour and to soften it. I have ordered this dish in quite a few Chinese restaurants, and, much better, in a Vietnamese one too. They were all quite different, so I consulted the internet and browsed through a few online recipes. This is what I came up with after a couple of attempts.

For 2   **20 minutes** **2 hours 30 minutes**

400–500g of pork belly

Half a cinnamon stick

1 star anise

A good chunk of ginger

3–4 garlic cloves

4–5 spring onions, chopped into inch-long pieces

1 tsp brown sugar (preferably coconut or similar)

½ cup Shaoxing wine

½ cup soy

Cut the belly into bite-size pieces and then place in a saucepan and cover with water. Bring to the boil and simmer for 15 minutes.

Blend the garlic and ginger or chop finely. Put in a second saucepan with a splash of oil and fry till they are softened. Add the rest of the ingredients and bring to the boil.

Add the belly back in. Add some stock or water from the first pan if you have none, and cover the belly. This lot should simmer away for at least two to three hours, by which time it's all reduced and the belly is softened, giving off a lovely aroma. Make sure it does not reduce too much!

There is another variation, equally good! The belly is cut into strips and placed in a large sheet of foil, along with whatever spices, fresh or dried, you want to add. The whole lot is wrapped in the foil, placed on a tray and baked on a low heat (say, 140°C) for a couple of hours. Then the liquid that has gathered is poured into a saucepan and the meat popped back in the oven again with sauce or fresh ginger and garlic added to crisp the belly. The liquid is reduced with added stuff like a little recap manis to make a sauce to add to the cooked belly. I favour ginger, garlic, and chipotle chilli sauce with the baked belly and then add a little more chipotle to finish.

Both versions are great served with rice and veg.

Braised Thai Chicken

An all-year-round winner: full of flavour, and great served with sticky rice and veg. I have to admit I have just mixed up a few recipes here! I love the idea but not so much the complexity of some of the lovely-tasting (I am sure) recipes I have read. Like most curries and Asian dishes, a pestle and mortar and a small to medium blender is essential really. In this recipe, you just need the blender. None of this equipment is at all expensive; they're just a bit more clutter in those already packed cupboards.

2 chicken legs or 4 thighs

Paste:

1–2 sticks of lemon grass

A good chunk of ginger

A large mild red chilli or two

4–6 garlic cloves

2 shallots (or failing that, 1 onion)

A large piece of fresh turmeric, dried (equivalent to about 2 teaspoons)

2–3 lime leaves

About 2 tablespoons of peanut, sesame or coconut oil (healthy oil!)

Ground salt and pepper

I teaspoon of coconut sugar

To add later:

2 whole star anise

8–10 curry leaves

When the paste is blending away, add oil bit by bit if you need to, to get a good consistency. Not runny but not too thick. Put it in a good size saucepan with a well fitting lid and gently fry it all, stirring a lot to stop it browning or burning. You may need a little more oil (I sometimes pour a little coconut milk in). This takes a few minutes and when it smells lovely it's time to tip half a can of coconut milk in and a couple of whole star anise and some curry leaves, which you remove before serving. So stir it all, and let this lovely liquid mix come to a simmer and drop in your fried/well browned chicken. It does not need to totally cover the chicken but near enough. You may need to add some more coconut milk or a little water. So, still simmering, pop the lid on with a good fit and relax.

This will cook really well in 75–90 minutes. Keep an eye on it, stir occasionally and if it reduces too much, pour a little water in and replace the lid.

Serve it all to the table in a big bowl, pour some of the liquid over your rice (any sort is fine). Serve with Asian kale or similar, maybe a little kimchi on the side or a teaspoon or two of pickled Asian veg.

My Dhal

I have been making this ever since my love of curry set in! I read quite a few recipes and decided I could mix them up and simplify it. I always make a pot full as it's just as easy to make a whole pot as a half, and it freezes very well – you could even say it's better the second time around!

For 3–4   **45 minutes**   **1 hour 15 minutes**

1 medium onion

4–5 garlic cloves

A half-teaspoon of dried chilli flakes

1½ teaspoons of cumin, freshly toasted and ground

1½ teaspoons of coriander, freshly toasted and ground

1 teaspoon of turmeric

4–5 cardamom pods

2–3 bay leaves

8–10 curry leaves (buy these fresh and remove the stalk and freeze to keep)

About 100–125g of chana dhal

200g of red split lentils

Salt and pepper to taste

Put the chana dhal in a bowl and soak for a couple of hours then simmer for at least 45 minutes. Meanwhile, toast the cumin, coriander and cardamom – dhal seems to benefit greatly from butter. Melt the butter then add the onion and garlic, fry gently till it's all soft. Add the ground spices, turmeric and chilli, and gently fry for a good 5 minutes or more. When it's fragrant, grind in salt and pepper.

Now add the red lentils to the now quite dry pan and stir them well, coating and mixing thoroughly. Add boiling water to cover, plus a couple of inches, then add the simmered chana dhal, curry leaves and bay leaves. As soon as this comes to the boil, simmer, stirring regularly, for about on hour, or until the lentils are soft. Turn it off and let it stand.

Reheat for 10 minutes or so, stirring occasionally, as otherwise it will stick when your meal is ready to eat.

Before taking it to the table, it adds to the appearance and taste to add some chopped coriander, a few thin slices of mild red chilli and chopped fresh tomato.

The other thing I like is to add in quite a lot of freshly washed spinach leaves and mix in while still simmering and when it's all wilted down. Pop it in a serving dish with the aforementioned additions.

Chana Masala

How many times have I ordered this with a takeaway! Hundreds maybe, and almost always with a chicken dansak, which I do love too. The dansak recipe in this book (page 53) reminds me of one I had in Mombasa many moons ago. That was really hot, and mine is more medium. The restaurant back then, in what was still a ramshackle city based upon its port and trade, was truly exotic to me and the friends I was working with. Everything was pungent with aromas and flavours and each dish was scattered with leaves, sticks and seeds. Truly memorable. The methi powder added to this chana is a poor replacement for fresh methi sprinkled on our Mombasa dish, though the real thing is very difficult to source. It is occasionally found in some of the London districts I have frequented.

For 6 — **15 minutes** — **1 hour 45 minutes**

2 cups of dried chickpeas (soaked overnight and simmered for 90 minutes)

1½ tsp coriander seeds

1½ tsp cumin seeds

5–6 cardamon seeds

5–6 cloves

1 large onion

1 good sized chunk of ginger

6–8 cloves of garlic

1 good sized piece of turmeric root

Oil (to blend)

1 tsp garam masala

Half a cinnamon stick

1 tsp paprika

1 can chopped tomatoes

Salt and pepper

With a little oil in a good size saucepan, fry the smooth blended stuff and add the toasted and ground seeds. On a low heat, stir and gently fry. Add the garam masala, cinnamon and paprika and continue till it's all fragrant and blended – about 10–12 minutes. Add salt and pepper and the tin of tomatoes and mix well. Simmer this lot for 15 minutes.

Then add the chickpeas and water to cover. Simmer for 80–90 minutes. The sauce in the pot will be reduced while still coating the chickpeas. Taste and season. When you have done so, add the methi and 2 teaspoons of coconut sugar, and simmer for 15 minutes.

That's it! Turn it into a large serving bowl. Sprinkle with chopped fresh coriander, chopped tomato and finely sliced mild red chilli. What's not eaten, put into a pot and pop it in the freezer for another day.

My Beetroot Curry

This is my attempt at cooking a very tasty dish served up in Sri Lanka where the curries are truly superb. It's no surprise, as the climate is warm and moist, with regular and plentiful rainfall interspersed by hot sunshine. So all the spices and vegetables grow strong and fast. This is a really rich, strongly flavoured curry and you do not need large portions. As with most curries, it freezes well.

For 4   45 minutes

2–3 good size beetroots	½ tsp fennel seeds
1 medium shallot	4–5 cloves
3–4 garlic cloves	½ tsp cinnamon
A small chunk of ginger	½ tablespoon desiccated coconut
A bigger chunk of fresh turmeric	2 tbsp oil
1 large mild red chilli	⅓ tin coconut milk
1 tsp coriander seeds	Salt and pepper
1 tsp cumin seeds	

Put all the fresh stuff – shallot, garlic, ginger, turmeric, etc. – and 1 tbsp oil in the blender and blend well. As always, the precise amount of oil to get the right consistency here is for you to judge: just do not start with too much, as you cannot remove it!

Put the seeds and cloves in a pan and toast gently till the mixture begins to turn. Grind it all in a pestle and mortar. Take a medium saucepan, add a tablespoon of oil and add the paste and the ground seeds and cinnamon, stirring all the while on a low heat.

When it's fragrant, add some of the coconut milk and some water and the desiccated coconut too, plus salt and pepper, then finally the beetroot chopped into chunks. Bring to the boil and simmer for at least 45 minutes, adding a little more coconut milk if required. Do not expect the beetroot to be soft – this takes a very long while – but by now it will be firm, yet easy to eat, and surrounded by a dark red, flavoursome sauce.

Dress with freshly chopped garlic cloves.

MY LOCKDOWN COOKBOOK

Cauliflower and Ginger Curry

Such a great dish for cauliflower lovers. It's got sauce to be soaked up by your choice of breads and rice, too. This is a big favourite in my house!

For 2   50/55 minutes

Half a medium cauliflower

1 stick of lemongrass

1 big chunk of ginger

1 shallot

About 10 curry leaves

1 tsp mustard seeds

2 tsp coriander

1 tsp turmeric

I tsp mild curry powder

Half a tin of coconut milk

Toast and grind the coriander seeds. Blend the ginger, turmeric and shallot with some oil. (Blending is optional! You can finely chop it all instead.)

Pour a little coconut oil in a medium saucepan and add the mustard seeds. On a low heat, pop the lid on and when you hear the seeds jumping about in the pan, add the blended shallot, ginger and turmeric. Fry gently for a few minutes then add the spices and fry till fragrant. Season with salt and pepper.

Add the coconut milk and curry leaves and bruised lemongrass. Simmer for 30 minutes: this will produce a thick, fragrant, tasty sauce.

Cut the cauliflower into big chunks and then place them in the pan: you may need a little water to loosen and thin the sauce. Put the lid on and simmer for 12–15 minutes, depending on how soft you like your cauliflower.

Turn it all into a serving bowl and sprinkle with chopped fresh coriander.

Twice Cooked Asian Chicken

Another experiment some purists will raise an eyebrow at. It does taste good, though, and that's according to a lover of Far Eastern food and a traveller many times to the region. I had something like this in Kuala Lumpur many moons ago. It was so good I ordered it three times in a 10-day stay. This is the nearest I have got and I now do it quite a few times a year. It works really well using a whole spatchcock chicken. You may need to consult the internet to spatchcock your chicken! It's not that difficult: just cut the bird in half, thus splitting it into two pieces, each with a breast, leg and wing.

This quantity will work for a small chicken, say just over 1 kilo. For three people, if you do a larger chicken, you will need to increase the quantities and choose a big enough saucepan.

15 minutes   **1 hour 45 minutes**

Small chicken (approx. 1 kg), spatchcocked

Paste:

A few shallots or 1 large onion

A large chunk of ginger

A large chunk of turmeric

A few garlic cloves

2 or more mild red chillies (depending on how hot you want it)

Some sort of oil (peanut, olive, coconut, etc.)

2 teaspoons cumin seeds, roasted and ground

1 teaspoon coriander seeds, roasted and ground

5–7 cloves

Half a cinnamon stick

Blend the onion, ginger and turmeric together. Add the ground spices to the blended stuff and fry gently in some more coconut oil. When it's all lovely and fragrant, pour in a can of coconut milk. Bring to a simmer.

Add the chicken. Be sure it's almost covered, so you may need more coconut milk or a some water, then put the lid on. Check every so often that it's not reducing too much; if it is, add a bit more coconut milk or some water. Simmer away for 90 minutes.

When that's done, choose an oven dish/tray that's the right size for the chicken. Then pick a small cup, add 1 tablespoon of Sambal Olek, 1 of Kitjap Manis and 1 of honey. Stir it all together and then brush all over the chicken halves. Place the chicken in a fan oven at 210–220°C. It should crisp the chicken's skin quite readily and only takes 10-15 minutes at most. Keep an eye on it so it does not blacken. Serve with a jug of the liquid to pour over your rice and some Asian greens.

Lamb Biryani

Considered by aficionados to be one of the best Indian dishes, if not the best. This recipe owes a lot to Meera Sodha, because hers was the first I found that seemed doable at home. With quite a few changes to her original, I have cooked this for many friends. I think it is one of the best too, and quite an impressive dish to serve at home.

For the dish to work you need a clay pot! Easy to find on the web: mine (shown below) was £25 and is the perfect size for four people. This earthenware pot is perfect for the biryani and makes all the difference. It's almost impossible to make a good biryani without one.

Prepare the pot before use by filling it with water and turning the lid upside down so it sits in the water too. It takes a while for the pot to darken, and this tells you it's ready to use. Pour the now cold water away and then fill with hot from the tap. Once this has heated the pot, empty again and follow the recipe.

For 4 · **30 minutes** · **3 hours 15 minutes**

1 star anise	6 cardamom seeds
2 large onions	1 heaped tbsp tomato purée
1 tbsp coriander seeds	½ tsp fennel seeds
A thumb-size piece of ginger	5 cloves
½ tablespoon cumin seeds	Small cinnamon stick
4–5 garlic cloves	600–700g lamb leg
20 black peppercorns	Generous grinding of sea salt
A thumb-size piece of turmeric	A large pinch of saffron
½ tsp dried chilli	Olive oil
1 heaped tbsp yoghurt	

Toast all the seeds together and then grind thoroughly. Blend all the soft stuff together, using only one of the onions.

Take a large saucepan and fry the powder in oil for quite a few minutes till it's really fragrant, then add the chopped lamb leg and fry on quite a high heat till it turns brown. Then add the blended stuff and stir till it's bubbling a little. Then cover with boiling water – make sure the water is at least an inch above the rest – add salt and put the lid on and simmer for 2½ hours. Check regularly and be sure to add water before it gets too thick; it should remain liquid. When the lamb is thoroughly softened and the liquid is dark and rich, turn off the heat.

Then cook basmati rice for four. (I prefer brown basmati.) At the same time, caramelise the remaining onion.

Having prepared your clay pot, start by spooning some lamb without the gravy into the bottom, then a layer of rice and then the caramelised onions, and repeat a few times so it's all layered and comes to within an inch of the top of the pot. Soak the saffron in hot water for 10–15 minutes and sprinkle on the top, then place the lid on and put it in the oven for 25 minutes at 175°C.

When it's done, serve at the table with the rich sauce in a jug, a bowl of garlic cucumber raita and coriander garnish if you like.

Squash and/or Courgette Curry

Quite a favourite in my house. This is simplified from the original: originally it was just a squash curry, but experimentation showed that it works well with courgette too, on its own or mixed with squash. Also, the tomato sauce without these veg can work as the basis for many veggies. If you're like us, you'll think the tomato sauce is almost the best bit! I have tried it with beetroot, various cabbages and potatoes.

For 4   **15 minutes**   **45 minutes**

1 mid size butternut squash (or other variety of squash – they all seem to work)

2 large or 3 mid-size courgettes

1 tsp cumin seeds

1 ½ tsp coriander seeds

½ tsp fennel seeds

2–3 cloves

1 good size shallot

4–5 garlic cloves

1 small chunk of ginger

1 small chunk of fresh turmeric

⅓–½ tsp chilli flakes

Salt and pepper

1 tin of chopped tomatoes.

Peanut, olive or coconut oil

Put all the fresh stuff in the blender and all the seeds and cloves in a pan to toast.

Put them both together in a medium-size saucepan with some oil and gently fry it all. Stir regularly and when it's fragrant add salt pepper and then the tin of tomatoes. Stir well and bring to the boil and reduce to simmer. Simmer for 45 minutes, adding a little water when needed. By the end it should be quite thick.

Whilst the sauce is simmering, peel the squash, remove the seeds and chop into bite-size pieces. Take an oven tray, cover with paper and put the squash on, spread it out and place in the oven at 200°C for 30–35 minutes.

If you want to add courgettes, or have all courgettes, top and tail, then cut into 2-inch chunks and then cut each chunk into half-inch-thick slices and place on a griddle. Add a mixture or whatever you decide to a serving bowl and cover with the sauce.

Dress with chopped garlic chives.

Kedgeree

This dish was originally invented by chefs in India for their British overlords rather a long while ago now. It was a dish that featured egg and was only lightly spiced so considered suitable as breakfast for the bland tastebuds of those needing service and sustenance. It became remarkably popular and is still served in many places worldwide. It really is a great dish, despite its questionable history! I love it as a light supper with some sort of chutney and maybe a samosa or two on the side.

For 2   **10 minutes**   **35 minutes**

Basmati rice

300g of smoked fish (haddock or cod are perfect)

2 large eggs (I love Burford browns, tastiest eggs around)

100–150g frozen peas

1 large onion

2–3 garlic cloves

A small chunk of ginger

2–3 cloves of cardamom

3–4 cloves

Fresh mild curry powder

½ teaspoon turmeric powder

Milk

Bay leaves

Fresh coriander and mint

Salt and pepper

The important thing is to put all the disparate parts together on a serving dish at the same time, ready to eat. So it's essentially a portion of spiced rice for two, flaked smoked fish, two soft boiled peeled eggs and frozen peas, garnished with a good handful of finely chopped fresh coriander and mint.

So, the spiced rice takes the longest and everything else should be timed around it.

Take a small to medium saucepan with a good fitting lid and fry the finely chopped onion garlic and ginger in some butter or coconut oil. After a few minutes, when it's all softened, add 2 teaspoons of fresh mild curry powder and turmeric, the cardamom seeds and a few cloves, plus salt and pepper. Fry it all gently for 7–10 minutes.

Then add the basmati rice and then one and a half times the quantity of water and bring to the boil. Add a couple of bay leaves, stir well and then place the lid on and turn the heat down to simmer for 10 minutes. Leave to stand for at least 5 minutes with the lid on.

At the same time, put the fish in another pan, with milk and water to almost cover it, plus a bay leaf or two and pepper. Simmer for 10 minutes, then take the fish out of the pan. Remove the skin and flake the fish with a fork. Boil the peas and boil the eggs for 6–7 minutes.

Take a serving bowl, pile the rice in first and then add the flaked fish and peas. Mix well, then place the soft boiled eggs quartered on the top and sprinkle the fresh herbs all over. Provide fresh cut lemons to squeeze on the side. Simple, healthy and delicious.

Sweet Potato and Coconut Curry

These kinds of dishes can be seen as side veggie dishes, or a healthy lunch or easy supper with rice, naan or flatbreads and maybe a samosa on the side.

For 2 as a main   **30/40 minutes**

1 tsp cumin seeds, toasted and ground

2 tsp mild curry powder

1 large fresh red chilli (remove seeds if you want it mild)

Salt and pepper to taste

1 large/medium onion

2 cloves of garlic, crushed or finely chopped

A thumb-size piece of ginger, finely sliced/chopped

2 good size tomatoes

250/300g sweet potatoes

150g spinach

Half a can coconut milk

Half the juice of a small lime

Pour some oil into a pot and add the well-chopped onion, garlic and ginger. Fry gently till nice and soft, then add the cumin, curry powder, chilli and salt and pepper. Fry gently till fragrant. Then add the chopped tomato and continue to fry till it's well mixed.

Add the coconut milk and potatoes and pop the lid on after bringing to the boil. Simmer till the potatoes are soft, then add the spinach and mix it in so that it wilts down.

Finally, before serving, add the lime juice and stir in and then tip it all into a serving bowl and sprinkle with fresh chopped coriander and mint.

Chinese Cabbage & Other Veg

Cooking any veg in the Chinese style can and should be quick and simple.

I prefer to taste the cabbage or whatever I am cooking. So this recipe is the way I cook the cabbage Koreans make into kimchi, and it works for pak choi, tat soi, choi sum and others.

Be sure it's fresh, and remember: all these sorts of vegetable cook down to look a lot less than you start with. Nothing on the scale of spinach, however. So a whole Chinese cabbage will serve four to five people. Use that as a guide in terms of weight per person.

Chinese Cabbage

5 minutes   5 minutes

So, for all these, get a big board and a sharp knife and slice/chop so that it's all ending up as a pile of smallish inch-long bits. Next if you like garlic, peel 2–4 cloves and slice/chop so that you have lots of little weeny bits.

Pop the wok on low heat, add a little oil – I use peanut oil – and pop the weeny bits of garlic in. Let them start to brown, then chuck all the chopped veg in. Turn the heat up full and add about two tablespoons of water and stir regularly. When the stalks have started to soften, and the liquid has evaporated, turn the heat down and add about 2–3 teaspoons of kekap manis and stir in for a couple of minutes.

Turn into a serving bowl and dress with a couple of teaspoons of toasted sesame seeds or finely sliced mild red chilli or both!

Kekap manis is a good thing to have in the cupboard. Often called Asian ketchup, it's cheap and quite thick and adds a slight sweet-salty flavour. Store in the fridge when open.

Choi sum

Chinese Chicken and Sweet and Sour Pork

Chinese Chicken

Sweet and Sour Pork

Here are two old favourites. The sweet and sour pork is my copy of a dish that was served in a Vietnamese café in Kilburn some 30 tears ago. What is loosely called Chinese chicken is something from a long ago trip to Taiwan! A kind and friendly bunch of teachers took us (TV crew plus director and presenter) to a local restaurant where local dishes came fast from the kitchen. Quite amusing, really, as first was a lovely soup, then this chicken or a bit like this, by which point we were all thinking that Taiwanese food was none too hot, but tasty. So, next came what was a traditional dish: dried whole chillies with chicken. Well, I have not to this day ever had anything quite so hot. But, since the teachers were all grinning and looking for our reaction, we all grinned back pretending it was no worry at all. Eventually the red faces and perspiration gave us away, and we all laughed and drank more beer!

| For 2 | 5 minutes | 10 minutes (both dishes) |

Chinese chicken:

300/400g chicken breast or deboned thigh, chopped to bite-size (works with duck breast too!)

Soy sauce

Mirin sauce

A big chunk of ginger

Sweet and sour pork:

300/400g pork fillet

A lot of ground pepper

Chinese rice vinegar

Coconut sugar or similar

Soy and fish sauce

1 large onion

Chinese Chicken

Chop the chicken, put in a bowl with finely chopped ginger, and then equal quantities of soy and mirin till the meat is almost covered. Put it in the fridge for a few hours. When ready, wok fry on high heat, turning regularly.

Sweet and Sour Pork

Take the pork to a board, remove the fatty bits, and slice to ½ cm thick. Spread it out and grind lots of pepper on to it. Heat your wok till the oil you pour in is smoky, then add the pork. On the highest heat, brown it quickly till it's cooked enough – about 4–5 minutes – then set aside in a serving bowl.

Cut the onion in half then into thin slices, put a little oil in the previously used wok and put all the onion in and fry hot and fast. When it's soft and beginning to brown, turn the heat right down. Add half a cup of Chinese rice vinegar, then a couple of level tablespoons of sugar and mix well on a low heat. Add just a couple of teaspoons of soy and 1 of fish sauce and stir.

Before serving, taste it! If you think it's too sweet or too sour, add a little something to combat this. Tip it all out on top of the pork. Chop a little fresh coriander as a garnish and serve.

Chinese Green Beans

There are usually two different sorts of beans in supermarkets. Preferably, these should be the ones labelled fine green beans. They are crisper and better flavoured, whilst the others – we can call them 'ordinary', as they are – have tougher skin and less flavour. If you have an East Asian grocer nearby, then you will have an even wider choice.

For 2 **10–15 minutes max**

250–300g fine green beans (or 140–160g if not the sole veg)

1 heaped tsp of sambal olek

1 tbsp of Shaoxing rice wine

½ tbsp of soy sauce

Start by washing the beans. Then top and tail. Then, cut them all into 1½–2 cm pieces. Put them in a saucepan and boil for a couple of minutes only, then drain and set aside. Next, take 1 good size shallot for every two servings and 2–3 garlic cloves: chop these finely and set aside.

Pop the wok on to medium heat and add some oil. Add all the onion and garlic and fry and stir for a few minutes, then turn up the heat and add all the beans. Stir regularly so that it's all well mixed. After another few minutes, add a heaped teaspoon of sambal olek per serving. Stir this in and you will have a fairly dry dish, so now add a tablespoon of Shaoxing rice wine and half a tablespoon of soy. Still on high heat, stir for another minute or two and turn into a serving bowl.

Dress with finely chopped coriander leaves.

Sambal olek is another common ingredient: it's essentially mushed up chillies. Bought in medium-size jars and kept in the fridge, it's useful and does enable you to determine the degree of heat. Handy, really, because chillies can vary so much and it can be frustrating trying to control how hot your dish is. Store the sambal olek in the fridge when open.

Shaoxing rice wine, used in many East Asian dishes, just gives that extra flavour, much in the way adding a splash of red wine does to a tomato sauce. Another bottle to keep in the cupboard.

Turmeric Chicken

I had this in a Thai restaurant in New York quite a few years ago. I searched and searched for a recipe right at the start of Lockdown, and eventually found one that I simplified down to this. The ingredients are easy to get now. 'Thai Food Online' (www.thai-food-online.co.uk) will have all of this, except sometimes the pandan leaves, but you can get them dried online in quite a few places. Coconut milk is best in tins; avoid the low fat version as it's not good! Prices for a tin vary from 59p in Lidl to over £2 in some supermarkets and delis, so shop around!

For 2   15 minutes   30 minutes

3 de-boned chicken thighs

For the paste:

75–80g fresh turmeric

50–60g shallots (Asian shallots: small yet strong-flavoured)

2 sticks of lemongrass

4–6 garlic cloves

Ground pepper

Peanut, olive or coconut oil (or any healthy oil really)

Salt and pepper to season

Pour the paste in a saucepan and fry gently. Once it starts to smell good, add the diced chicken meat and fry gently till the oil starts to separate out. Then add a little coconut milk – about one-third of a can should do – and some pandan leaves, about half a teaspoon of the dried ones. This needs to bubble away gently for 20 minutes or so.

It's a very good dish if your tummy needs to settle. It's tasty and easy.

Serve with kimchi for even better digestion, some sort of rice and a veg or two, plus my ever-pleasing Asian pickled veg.

Chicken Dansak

This dish is the takeaway curry dish I was always ordering but never managed to find a recipe that was in any way similar. Dansak is more Persian than Indian, but that's not the issue here at all. None of the great books I mentioned previously went anywhere near this recipe and it was only in Lockdown, after quite a few attempts, that I got to this. If, like me, you love a good dansak, try it!

For 3–4   **1 hour**   **30 minutes**

2 large chicken breasts or 3 good boneless chicken thighs

2–3 medium onions

Thumb-size chunk of ginger

4–5 garlic cloves

Finger-size chunk of turmeric

1 tbsp tomato paste

Juice of half a lemon

2 tsp coconut or palm sugar

3–4 cardamom seeds

1 tsp methi powder or fresh leaves

1 tsp Madras powder

½ tsp garam masala

½–1 tsp chilli flakes

1 cinnamon stick

2–3 bay leaves

Generous grinding of sea salt and black pepper

100g split peas/lentils (simmered for 60 minutes)

Start by washing lentils and then simmering. As this is going on, blend the top section of fresh spices. Roast and grind the cardamom seeds.

In a medium-size saucepan, pour in a few tablespoons of peanut, coconut or mustard oil and add the blended spices. Fry gently. Add the ground cardamom and the other dry spices (except the cinnamon stick) as it's frying, plus the salt and pepper. Fry for a good 10 minutes, stirring regularly.

Then add the chicken chopped into mouth-sized pieces and continue to fry. When the chicken has changed colour and everything is fragrant, add the lentils and some water to cover, plus the bay leaves. This should simmer away and become a very saucy curry, done when the lentils are soft!

Garnish with chopped tomato and chopped fresh coriander, and serve with rice, naan and veg of your choice or chana dhal. Lovely!

This is mild to medium: personally, I prefer medium for this. More chilli!

Japanese Cucumber Salad

This is a simple and typical Japanese dish: clean flavour, fresh on the palate, healthy. It goes with any old Japanese and many East Asian meals. Made with a very sharp knife it's just fine. However, I started making this obsessively, so we bought a spiraliser. This gadget makes a really interesting improvement, as the cucumber is slightly thinner and in a long piece – like peeling an apple, only much longer. Looks good on the table, too.

MY LOCKDOWN COOKBOOK

For 4   12-15 minutes

1 large or 2 smaller organic cucumbers

Japanese rice vinegar

Sugar (e.g. organic coconut)

Mirin

Salt (ground sea salt, obviously!)

Sesame seeds

Top and tail the cucumber. Then, with a hand peeler, peel long strips of the skin, leaving a gap, then another, so that when it's sliced it has striped edges. Then cut the cucumber lengthways and slice each half as thinly as possible, or spiralise if you have one. Pick the entire pile up and gently squeeze, dribbling the liquid/juice into a jug. Pop the cucumber into a serving bowl.

Next, take a tablespoon of sesame seeds and toast them slowly till they begin to turn in colour.

Next, pour half a cup of Japanese vinegar into the jug. Add a teaspoon of sugar, one of salt, and a tablespoon of mirin. Stir it all to dissolve the salt and sugar.

(All sugar has a slight character, from white processed through to organic cane or coconut. It all works, but I try to keep to the less industrialised versions. This does not work out too expensive in cooking meals, as it's usually the odd teaspoon here and there, not 8 ounces for every cake!)

So, take the jug with the liquid in and pour half over the cucumber. It should suck up some or all, then add more, till it's dressed, not drowned!

Finally, add the toasted sesame seeds, half stirred in and half sprinkled on the top. Serve. Or if it's to be eaten later, just shove it in the fridge and remove a little while before you want to eat it.

RECIPES FROM THE FAR EAST

55

Japanese Baked Salmon and Spinach

This is an old favourite. No idea where it came from. The simple salmon dish was possibly the hot main I often ordered in a little Japanese café in West Hampstead decades ago, when Japanese food was a rarity. The spinach part is a simplified recipe from a traditional cookbook that's been with me for ages. This can be rustled up in half an hour. So healthy and tasty too! Wild salmon is always best; farmed is fatty but still works well.

 For 2   15 minutes   15 minutes

2 pieces of salmon

3–4 tbsp Japanese soy sauce (preferably Kikkoman)

3–4 tbsp Japanese mirin sauce

A big chunk ginger

A medium size bag of spinach

Sesame seeds

Place the salmon pieces in an oven dish. Finely chop the ginger and spread it about the dish. Pour in equal amounts of the soy and mirin sauces, about 2–3 tablespoons. Mix it by tipping it gently side to side.

Cooking the salmon takes 15 minutes in the fan oven at 200°C. As soon as it is in the oven, put the rice on too so it's cooked at the same time.

Meanwhile, take the bag of fresh spinach and put it all into a medium saucepan. Add a little water, like half a cupful or so, and turn on a medium heat and put the lid on. After a couple of minutes the water will be boiling in the bottom, so mix it about to get the stuff on top down to the bottom and replace the lid. In a couple more minutes the entire pot will be wilted down and look like there's not so much at all!

Tip it through a sieve into a jug so the liquid is saved. Squeeze the spinach so that the remainder of the liquid goes into the jug. Put the small ball of spinach in a decent size bowl.

Now, toast a generous quantity of sesame seeds, then when they start to change colour, put them in a pestle and mortar and grind them. You need to stop before it's all ground so that there are still chunks of seed left.

Next, take the spinach liquid, discard nearly half of it, put the partly ground sesame seeds in, add about a tablespoon of mirin and soy. Stir again.

Take the bowl with your cooled spinach. With a sharp knife, holding the spinach in a sort of ball, cut through the spinach a few times. Now spread it out, then pour the liquid over it. The liquid will mostly be absorbed.

This is how I do it, and in that order. The first few times you make it, I suggest you cook the spinach before the salmon goes in the oven, and put the rice on at the same time as the salmon goes in to the preheated oven. With practice, this will be easy and quick and always enjoyable. After doing this a few times, you can confidently follow it in the order I do it, so it becomes that '30-minute meal'!

Korean Pork or Chicken

Korean food is yet another Far East style that's very different. It's where the kimchi comes from. I love pork belly, and could have included four or five recipes for scrumptious Asian or European dishes. I decided that, right now, this is my favourite.

For 2

15 minutes + marinade time   20 minutes

Korean chicken

500g of pork belly with the skin removed, sliced roughly into inch-thick pieces

2–3 garlic cloves

1 tablespoon of Korean Gochujang hot red pepper paste

I tablespoon of honey

1 tablespoon of soy

A large chunk of ginger

1 tablespoon of sesame seeds

The juice of half a good-size lime

Take a good size bowl and put the pork in and add all the liquids. Finely chop all the solids and add and mix thoroughly.

This is best done first thing in the morning or even the day before cooking. The longer you leave it, the better. The lime juice will soften the meat, whilst all the other strong flavours will be infused. Stir every so often.

Take a large frying pan. Pour in a little peanut oil or other good oil. Pick the pieces of pork out with tongs and pop them into the pan. Fry it all gently, turning every few minutes. This stuff spits on your splashback and hob, making a bit of a mess, while the honey in the mix can get a bit stuck to the pan. It's worth it!

After 12–13 minutes or so, when the pork pieces change colour and the fatty bits begin to darken, take your tongs and pick the meat out, putting it in a nice serving bowl.

The actual frying part takes about 12–15 minutes. Cleaning up after – well, how quickly can you clean? It's always quickest and easiest to clean immediately after you cook and before it's a dried-up, stuck-on mess! Don't be put off, though. I use a wok, and that stops a lot of the spitting. Try that if you too have a wok, or just use a frying pan and a gauze and do a little cleaning!

You can change the meat to chicken by using the same stuff, but leave out the honey. It's great with kimchi and veg, and pretty good too with noodles and beans.

Kale 'Oriental Style'

I have no evidence whatsoever that kale is grown or eaten in the Far East! It is, after all, a cold weather crop, but then China does have some pretty chilly zones. Anyway, I found this on some online cooking site, and it goes well with quite a few types of dish. I have had it with my favourite rendang and kimchi, which was good! Kale's just a fashion, some say. Others are quite disturbed that a crop grown as animal feed is now so popular with people. But it's supposed to be good for you and, anyway, I like it. Freshness is so important, I found out: the supermarkets chop it all up, including the stalk, then send it on some merry-go-round journey before it gets to a shelf, whereas my local farm shop picks it and sells it the next day, all crisp and fresh. In winter, they have green, purple and sometimes the frizzy, almost white stuff. I love the purple kale, which weirdly turns green when it's cooked. My farm shop's cavolo nero, which also works well here, is very different as it's so fresh. When I lived in London, just a few years ago, the fruit and veg shop in Crouch End was excellent and their stuff very fresh, so it's not impossible to make this in London.

MY LOCKDOWN COOKBOOK

For 2   **5 minutes**   **10-12 minutes**

Kale (use the amount you would
normally use)

1 tbsp sesame seeds

⅛ cup soy sauce

1 tsp coconut sugar

Whilst the kale is steaming or simmering, toast a good tablespoon of sesame seeds. Whilst that's happening, take a cup, add an eighth of a cup of soy and the same of water. Add one teaspoon of coconut sugar or your choice of sugar, then, when the seeds start to turn colour, spoon them into the cup and listen to the sizzle! Good that, because it's infusing it with flavour.

Now, when your kale is cooked, pour it through a sieve, losing all the liquid. With a wooden spoon, press what you can out of the kale. Turn the kale into a serving bowl and add the cup of dressing. Mix well so some is absorbed and it's ready to serve and eat.

What you will learn, as I have, is that cooking time really does vary with freshness and age and other issues too probably, so it might take a few goes to get the time right. Too long is better in this case than too short, as unlike many veg, kale is really robust and does not end up as a sludge!

Tom Yam and Tom Ka Soups

The bag of paste and the jar both easily make the best homemade Thai-style soup I have ever had. They are lovely and easy to make.

Tom yam soup

For 2   5 minutes   20 minutes

About 200ml of chicken stock

Some coconut milk

A couple of spring onions

Some Chinese cabbage

Mushrooms (optional)

Prawns (optional)

Whatever else you are inclined to add!

For the Tom Yam soup: Defrost your stock in a small/mid-size saucepan and bring to a simmer. Add 2 heaped teaspoons of the paste from the jar, and let it slowly mix in, stirring occasionally. Add about a third of a can of coconut milk and stir and simmer for a while.

Meanwhile, take 2 soup bowls and into each share a handful of finely chopped spring onion and a handful of Chinese cabbage chopped into ½-inch square pieces.

Once the soup has simmered for 15 minutes or so, you can add prawns or mushrooms and simmer for a few minutes longer till it's cooked through, then pour equally over the spring onion and cabbage in the bowls. Lovely!

For the Tom Ka soup from the paste: simply copy the above, but start with the paste. Cook for a few minutes and then slowly add the coconut milk and then the stock and simmer as before.

Roast Spiced Cauliflower

This is lovely. Simple and quick, too. You will find many recipes that work for this, and often the same basic ingredients are there, just in different quantities.

Homemade curry is great once you have got the knack! It's good, presentation-wise and for variety, to have some items that are in a sauce and some without, and vary the colour and texture too. So I will do a rich lamb curry, much like the one we start a biryani with, then make this cauliflower on the side, maybe a cucumber raita or a bowl of dhal, all served with rice or naan. This recipe is for two to three people – although some cauliflower fans eat a lot!

MY LOCKDOWN COOKBOOK

 **For 2–3** **20 minutes** **30-40 minutes**

Half a large cauliflower, broken into small pieces.

2 teaspoons of freshly toasted cumin seeds

Ground sea salt

Half a teaspoon of turmeric

Half a lemon or lime squeezed

Chilli or cayenne to taste

2 tablespoons of olive oil or some other oil – but not coconut, it's too strong

Put all the pieces of cauliflower in a big bowl. Do not make them too small, as cooking does shrink them.

Grind the cumin seeds once toasted in a pestle and mortar. Add the sea salt and ensure that's ground in too, then add the rest and stir it all. Turn it all into the big bowl with the cauliflower and mix it thoroughly – and then some!

Then turn the mixture into a non-stick oven tray, spread it evenly and put it in the fan oven at 210°C for 30 minutes or until it's all getting browned. By this time, it will have shrunk substantially and be a little crisp.

My Spring Rolls

I can safely admit that, when I emerged from Norfolk as a teenager ready for
college, Chinese food was exotic and irresistible. To begin with, spring rolls
were filled with angel hair noodles and grated carrot and cabbage. Eventually,
these humble beginnings became an explosion of different flavours, filled with
seafood, meat and interesting veg and herbs. So my spring rolls are the best I
can do to copy what was served in a family-run corner eatery in San Francisco.
My friend Jeff and I went to this spot every evening for six days as it was a
two-minute walk from our hotel. After two days trying many different and
tasty things, on the third day we asked the chef to cook us stuff he and his
family would eat. These spring rolls were the most memorable and many of the
dishes had ingredients I had never seen or tasted, so it was a great end to many
busy working days. I realise my description of how to roll these little delights
may not be so good. So I strongly suggest you find a YouTube tutorial, of which
there are plenty. It's not difficult at all. Eat them dipped in sweet chilli sauce
with soy or whatever you want to try.

MY LOCKDOWN COOKBOOK

1 pack of medium-size spring roll cases

10/12 uncooked large prawns, peeled

4/5 crab sticks (or real crab meat – much better, but pricey!)

2/3 spring onions

A large chunk of ginger

Chop the prawns, crab-sticks (or crab), spring onions and ginger finely. Pop it all in a bowl.

Open the thawed spring roll cases and peel off the top one. Put on the work surface in front of you. Take about a sixth of the mixture and place it near a corner of the pastry case. Now take the corner of the pastry and move it across the mix. Start to roll it gently; after a turn, fold the left and right parts of the pastry over the roll, continue to roll until the pastry is all rolled, leaving a corner.

In a small cup, add a couple of teaspoons of cornflour and add a little water. Stir to make a sloppy paste, adding a bit more of either to get it the right consistency. This is your glue, so use a brush, dipped in the paste, to coat the final half a turn of the pastry generously, then finish rolling tightly. Set aside to dry, and repeat. You should make 6 rolls from this mix.

Now that I happily own a hot air fryer, I spray the spring rolls with oil and pop them in for 15–20 minutes at about 190°C, or till they are slightly browned all over. Could be more than 20 minutes: just turn them once or twice and be sure they are beginning to brown. Or deep fry for much less time.

Asian Beef Short Rib

This is a truly amazing dish! It's not quick at all, but it does make a really tremendous meal for guests, or a special treat – one of those really impressive, big dishes that arrives at the table to oohs and ahhs and even the odd wow! It takes a few hours too, so get it all in the oven well before your guests arrive.

For 4   15 minutes   3 hours

1.5–2 kg beef rib, chopped into 4–5 inch chunks by the butcher

1 good size onion

4–5 garlic cloves

A big chunk of ginger

3 whole star anise

1 tsp coriander

1 tsp five spice

½ tsp cayenne pepper

½ tsp black pepper

2 tbsp soy sauce

3 tbsp rice wine

3 tbsp rice vinegar

Fresh mint, coriander and a large red chilli to garnish

Salt and pepper to season

Roast the seeds and grind to a powder. Blend the soft stuff with a little oil. Fry the ribs till they begin to turn brown and set aside.

Take a large casserole with a well-fitting lid, add a little oil, add the blended stuff and the ground spices, fry till fragrant, then slowly add the soy, wine and vinegar, plus the star anise. Stir well and bring to simmer, then pop the ribs all in. If you have any stock handy, add 100–200 ml; if you have none, then add about 300 ml water.

Put the lid on and place in the oven at about 140°C for about three hours! Check occasionally to be sure the pot does not reduce too fast. When all's done and you bring it to the table, you will want all the lovely juices to pour on your rice.

The dish has a wonderfully rich and yet subtle flavour, whilst the meat falls off the bone and is very tender. Serve with rice, a veg and maybe some kimchi.

Tikka Paste

This is another great paste that's easy to make and can be frozen in small containers ready to defrost for that barbecue or for quick grilled portions of lamb, chicken or fish.

1 big chunk of ginger

3–5 garlic cloves

2–3 mild red chillies

1 1/2 teaspoons cumin seeds

2–3 teaspoons coriander seeds

2 teaspoons of paprika

1 teaspoon of cayenne

3 teaspoons of Garam masala

A big squeeze of tomato paste, 3/4 tablespoon roughly

A big hand full of freshly washed coriander including the stalks

Juice of half a lime

1 shallot

2 tablespoons olive oil

Toast the cumin and coriander seeds, grind in your pestle and mortar.

Put the shallot, chilli, garlic and ginger in the blender along with the oil and the coriander leaves and purée. Blend to a nice liquid paste, then add all the dry spices. Blend, adding a little oil to ensure a good consistency.

Use what you need while fresh and freeze the remainder in little boxes/pots.

Malay Mixed Vegetable Pickle

Eating out in the UK's Asian restaurants, we rarely get served pickles, only in the more expensive £40–50 per head places. But if you are fortunate enough to travel and eat in the far east, pickles are very often served, and considered part of most main courses and often a decorative part of a starter too. These can be cooked in a large quantity and refrigerated. They last a long while when they are kept in the fridge with a tight fitting lid on. They are really nice on the side: crunchy, tasty and spicy.

500ml of pickling vinegar

1 unpeeled cucumber, cut into small strips or sticks

3 large carrots, cut into sticks, an inch or so long and a quarter inch thick.

Half a pound of white cabbage, finely chopped.

1 cauliflower, cut into small florets.

Mixed chillies, seeds removed, cut into strips

6 oz of Demerara sugar

10 ounces of roughly crushed peanuts

10 ounces of toasted sesame seeds

2 teaspoons turmeric

1 teaspoon chilli powder

6+ crushed chopped garlic cloves

1 teaspoon of ground sea salt

4–5 tablespoons peanut oil or other healthy oil

Put the vinegar in a saucepan and bring it to the boil. Scald the vegetables in batches for a minute or so each. Remove each batch with a sieve or netted basket and remove as much vinegar as possible. Put them in a big bowl. Then add the nuts and seeds. Finely chop the garlic and fry in a generous quantity of oil so it begins to brown. Add it all, oil included, to the bowl along with all the rest of the ingredients. Mix everything thoroughly and then spoon it into a large jar or a few small ones. The jars and lids must have been boiled gently in a pan with a little water to be sure they are fully sterilised. Do not touch the inside of the jar or lid, so use a wooden spoon to lift and manoeuvre.

Have a couple of teaspoons per person with most Asian meals. It last weeks, if not months, with a tight fitting lid in the fridge.

Near Eastern Food

One of the oldest known cookery books comes from the near East. Indeed, the early Iranian, Iraqi, Egyptian, Greek and Roman cultures are all truly ancient: over the centuries, the melting pot they represent has produced a wide and varied cuisine.

Takeaway kebabs were probably the first food I came across that was from this part of the world. Slowly, over the years, we have been educated in the very varied cuisines of the region, and today Yotam Ottolenghi's restaurants and cookbooks are very fashionable indeed. TV travel and food shows bring us tagines from Morocco that people travel miles to get to and then queue to sit and eat. It has been a recent thing for me, and something that for many years I wanted to explore. I now make tagines that are really tasty to eat and relatively easy to cook. It seems the combination of meat and fruit is quite normal, in a way that many of us who cook are not comfortable with at first. It's outside our comfort zone: we are used to thinking of fruit coming after the main course.

I still have so much to learn about Middle Eastern food. I have been fortunate to travel to Israel and Egypt, for example, and although they are neighbouring countries, their cuisines are very different.

Lamb, chicken and goat are the staples, combined with dates, figs, pistachio, pomegranate and apricot. Then onion, garlic, cinnamon, turmeric, cumin and nutmeg are added to achieve a fascinating balance of flavour. These dishes are cooked slowly, like our stews: in this case, this is done in a traditional clay pot called a tagine. I have yet to treat myself to one of these pretty earthenware pots as I, like many, have only so much space. I do, however, believe that cooking in a good solid saucepan with a well-fitting lid and a good thick base is almost as good.

Away from the tasty tagines, the Mediterranean and the Red Sea provide a very varied spread of fish, prawn, squid and more, and these are cooked in many unusual ways too. This is my next area of discovery: I now live near the sea, having left London a few years ago.

Moroccan Lamb Meatballs With Couscous Harissa

These meat balls are really full of flavour, and the couscous is different too. The creamy kefir yoghurt was good with this and a big pile of mixed leaves, cucumber, tomato and pomegranate seeds. Fresh and full flavoured!

For 4   **1 hour (with practice)**

For the meatballs:

400–500g minced lamb

1 large shallot or 1 medium onion,
finely chopped

2 cloves of garlic, crushed or minced

1 heaped teaspoon of ground cumin
(freshly toasted is best)

Half a teaspoon of coriander

Juice of half a lemon

1 tablespoon plain flour

Ground sea salt and generous
quantity of black pepper

Put it all in a bowl and mix thoroughly. Form it into 20–24 balls by pressing a small amount together and gently rolling it between your palms. Put the meatballs on a tray, cover and put in the fridge to set. An hour later, put them all in a frying pan and fry gently till browned all over.

MY LOCKDOWN COOKBOOK

For the couscous:
60–80g couscous per person
Chicken stock

Harissa paste
1 large shallot
Fresh mint leaves

Place the measured couscous in a good size bowl. Measure the stock depending on how many portions you are making. Add a teaspoon of harissa per person, bring to the boil and pour over the couscous in the bowl.

When it's fully done and has absorbed the stock – 10 minutes for wholewheat couscous and 5 for normal – finely chop a small shallot or onion and finely mince/chop a small pile of mint leaves and stir into the couscous.

Serve with creamy yoghurt and cucumber dish and salad of your choice. Fresh leaves are best, but only if really fresh ones are available!

Chicken and Preserved Lemon Tagine

Another 'happy tummy' dish that's full of flavour. I bought one of a plethora of healthy cookbooks some time ago and this was one of a few really tasty dishes I cooked repeatedly. I have simplified it and lost a few ingredients.

 **For 2**   **10 minutes**   **1 hour 20 minutes**

1–2 tablespoons of olive oil	1 teaspoon turmeric
1 onion diced	1 teaspoon paprika
4 chicken thighs	Half a preserved lemon
2 garlic cloves	A handful or 6–8 apricots, halved
A medium sized chunk of ginger, diced	Chopped fresh coriander
	Chicken stock – about 200ml
1 teaspoon cinnamon	Salt and pepper

In a suitable casserole, heat the oil, add the onion and garlic and fry for a few minutes. Add the chicken and brown it all over. Stir in the ginger and spices. Fry, stirring well. After a few minutes when it's fragrant, add the stock, the preserved lemon and the apricots. Pop the lid on and put it in the oven for well over an hour – maybe an hour and a half is enough – at 130–140°C.

When you are ready to eat, add the chopped coriander and stir it in.

Pretty easy and very healthy, especially for the tummy! Good with red rice, brown rice, couscous, etc.

Harissa Baked Chicken

A relatively recent addition to my repertoire that's become a real favourite. Never have potatoes been so tasty! It's all put in a bowl or bag after breakfast. Should not take long to prepare, maybe 10 minutes. Then it's a lovely easy quick dish to chuck in the oven on a tray and serve with salad in the summer and purple broccoli or your favourite greens in the winter. The number of potatoes can be varied, according to how hungry people are!

For 2   **prep: 10 minutes (max); cook: 1 hour**

4 thighs of 2 legs of chicken

Firm roasting potatoes, cut into a size that's about two mouthfuls (I like the dark red ones best)

A few tablespoons of nice plain yoghurt

A couple of tablespoons of olive oil

Some sea salt and black pepper

At least 1 teaspoon ground cumin (it really helps if you roast this freshly)

Zest of half a lemon

3–4 garlic cloves (chopped to good sized chunks, as they are going to roast to a crisp)

I tablespoon lemon juice

I tablespoon of harissa paste

So, place all the ingredients in a large bowl or bag in the fridge all day, massage it a couple of times or give it a good stir.

When it's time to cook, remove it all and spread over an oven tray so that it's all sort of separate. Place it in your fan oven at 190–200°C for 50/55 minutes or so.

I do repeat this, I know, but be aware all our ovens can cook differently at the same temperature. Keep an eye on it so the chicken skin crisps but does not burn.

Remove from the oven and stack it all in a serving dish.

Add the yoghurt to the top, and serve with your salad or veg.

If you have the time and like it, at the very end, add a half a cup of mixed chopped herbs with a couple of tablespoons of yoghurt and a squeeze of lemon or lime if you prefer. This can be spooned on top of the entire big bowl after cooking. I rarely bother with the topping as we love it as it is, but if I cook for guests I generally do… Adds a little something, I guess!

I have never had a recipe that marinates potatoes, but they are the best-tasting roasted potatoes ever. Love this dish: quick, easy and delicious.

Lamb Tagine

This is easy to cook in a saucepan – handy, as I do not have one of those pretty terracotta tagines to put in the oven. You can almost put it in the pot and leave it for the best part of an hour or so, simmering with the lid on between additions, as long as you have a very low setting on your cooker, as that's what it needs. If not, you'll need to pay it a little more attention, stirring and adding water if needed.

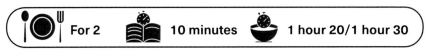

For 2   **10 minutes**   **1 hour 20/1 hour 30**

300–400g of leg meat, neck fillet or similar, chopped into chunks

1 big onion or a couple of good shallots

A big handful of semi-dried apricots

Ground salt and pepper

I big heaped teaspoon of cumin

1 flat teaspoon of cinnamon

1 flat teaspoon of turmeric

About 1 tablespoon of honey or pomegranate molasses (both these add sweetness: see which you prefer, as the flavour is different)

MY LOCKDOWN COOKBOOK

So tip some oil – I use olive oil or butter for this – into a saucepan. Add the chopped onion and fry till it's about to brown around the edges then add the lamb. Generally, I turn the heat up here to brown the meat rather than boil it! Do not worry when the pan gets burnt around the edges as this will dissolve into the juices.

Once you think it's started to brown nicely, add the spices, turn the heat down and stir it as the spices start to give off their fragrance (the fresher the spices the stronger that fragrance). Keep stirring away and add salt, pepper and the honey or molasses. Stir for a few minutes till it's even and in danger of sticking, and then cover with boiling water.

Once it's all boiling, turn it right down, scrape all the brown or burnt stuff of the sides, put the lid on and leave it.

After 45 minutes or so, add the apricots – be sure, again, it's got just enough water – put the lid back on and cook for another 45–60 minutes. Keep an eye on it: do not let it get too reduced. If it does, add more water.

You will know when it's done! Juicy, soft and smells lovely, sitting in a gravy that's dark and not watery.

Serve with rice, couscous, or flat breads if you can buy or even make them. My choice, if I have the time, is whole couscous, made with stock, with chopped up onion, mint and coriander thrown in with a little oil. Sometimes we have some sort of green with this. Maybe not traditional, but we live in the UK and we need to be healthy and enjoy it too.

I love lots of different veg, and it's always good for us to eat and easy to serve. In the summer I have had all sorts of salads too.

Lamb, Butternut Squash and Prune Tagine

This is yet another recipe from way back. Many moons ago an old friend, who was indeed Iranian, cooked this quite often. It was always served with spiced rice in a rice cooker, but I could never seem to remember the ingredients for that. In fact, the tagine only really came back to me recently while reading one of the many books on cooking I enjoy. Tagines are very flavourful and rarely spicy at all – just good fresh ingredients. Perfect for our cooler months, so more than half the year. They fill the house with a fragrance and aroma that makes my mouth water.

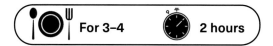

For 3–4　　**2 hours**

2 onions or shallots

400–500g lamb leg

2 tsp ground cumin

1 1/2 tsp ground cinnamon

1 heaped tsp turmeric

2 tbsp tamarind paste

2 tbsp honey or pomegranate molasses

1 small butternut squash

A good handful of semi-dried pitted prunes

Salt and pepper

Take a good size saucepan and pour in a few tablespoons of olive oil. On a slow or low heat, add the chopped shallots or onions and cook till soft and then add the lamb, chopped into good sized chunks. Be sure to turn up the heat and fry till the lamb begins to brown, then turn down again, adding in the spices, and cook till it's smelling lovely.

Add the tamarind and honey/pomegranate molasses. Stir well and season with generous salt and pepper and then cover with water. Simmer for at least an hour with the lid on.

Then add the peeled and deseeded chopped squash and the prunes and mix in well. Add a little more water if it's needed, then replace the lid and simmer again for 30–45 minutes. Do check it's not reducing too much during this period.

It should still have plenty of tasty liquid gravy and the squash should be soft but not squishy, then it's ready to serve.

Great with couscous, flat breads, rice and greens of your choice.

Braised Chicken with Figs

This dish was cooked for me by my friend Roy on one of our bridge nights a few years ago. It was a treat, so I asked him to email the recipe to me. It was originally from one of Ottolenghi's books. At first I used Roy's recipe to the letter but subsequently dropped some of the ingredients and simplified it. It's now a different dish all together.

For 2   **10 minutes**   **1 hour 20 minutes**

2 chicken legs or 4 thighs

2 decent sized shallots, or 3 smaller ones

3–4 garlic cloves

4–5 whole semi-dried figs

A large tablespoonful of fresh thyme

A handful of parsley

A couple of bay leaves

Salt and pepper

2 tablespoons of balsamic vinegar (or 2–3 tablespoons of red wine vinegar if you don't have balsamic)

1 tablespoon of pomegranate molasses

A good slosh of wine (optional)

This dish has to go in the oven. I use a round oven dish about 20cm across and 8 or so deep. Place the chicken in the pot with space around it. Fill in the gaps with shallots cut in half or quarter, garlic in chunks and the figs quartered.

Then add the herbs. Then the liquids. The liquids should almost cover the chicken, but not quite. If necessary, add some water. Hold the dish in your hands and move the mixture about. You want to mix it well, really well.

If you have time, leave it to stand for a while to infuse. If not, no worries; grind the salt and pepper over the chicken that's exposed. Then place in your fan oven at 190°C and cook for roughly 1 hour 15 minutes. Keep an eye on it: if it reduces too quickly, add water or wine. Be sure to mix the liquid in, but slowly so you do not wash over the chicken.

The chicken skin should be crispy and the liquid reduced by about a half. The meat will fall off the bone and the shallots will be translucent and soft.

I like this with roast potatoes, roast carrots and boiled or steamed greens.

Butter Bean, Kale and Squash Stew

This is a hearty and healthy dish. Lovely for a lunch time during the winter, and equally good as an evening meal, any time.

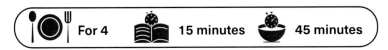 For 4   15 minutes   45 minutes

1 medium onion

4–6 garlic cloves

A big chunk of ginger

A big chunk of turmeric (or 1½ tsp ground if you have not got the fresh stuff)

Oil to blend and fry (coconut, mustard or olive oil are fine)

2 tsp coriander seeds

½ tsp cinnamon

½ tsp cayenne pepper

½ tsp sea salt

1 tbsp soy

½ kilo squash (I generally use butternut, as it's always available)

2 400g cans of butterbeans or 250g dried beans (soaked overnight, then boiled for about 45 minutes till softish)

1 can of coconut milk

150g kale, stalks removed and chopped

40–50g fresh coriander

Take a large saucepan and add some oil. Pop in all the blended soft ingredients and add the roasted ground coriander and other dry spices on a low heat for a good 7–10 minutes, till the fragrance is released.

Then add the soy and coconut milk, sea salt and pepper, and the beans and squash.

Cover with boiling water and simmer for 20 minutes or until the squash has softened.

Then add the kale and cook for a further 10/12 minutes, or if using spinach, cook for 5 minutes, and finally add the freshly chopped coriander and stir well.

Serve with flat breads or any bread of your choice.

It's fine to change the main ingredients of this recipe. We have come to prefer cauliflower, sweet potato and spinach (see picture below); the recipe for this can be made using the above instructions.

Warm Red Rice Salad with Courgette

I learnt this recipe when I was trying to make my tummy happier. Too much sugar and too much stress, and the biome gets out of whack. This 'tummy food' is tasty like other stuff with that label. I abhor eating tasteless or boring food to get healthy! There are so many ways and foods to help this process that are tasty – that's what I choose!

For 2 | **40 minutes** | **20 minutes**

120–140g of pre-cooked red rice

2 courgettes, sliced and halved

Half a small red cabbage with all the stalky stuff removed, chopped into bite-size bits

40g toasted pine nuts

Half a small preserved lemon, diced

2 tbsp olive oil

Juice of half a lemon

Chopped fresh parsley

Chopped fresh mint

Fresh thyme leaves

Warm the rice in the microwave and spoon it in to a serving bowl.

Put the courgette on a hot griddle, so it chars on both sides and softens.

Do the same with the red cabbage. Add them both to the rice and then the rest of the ingredients and stir it all together well.

Great with grilled or barbecued meat or fish. Good on its own for lunch.

Roast Beetroot and Yoghurt Dip

Discovered again when I was searching for 'tummy food'. This is great on the side with barbecued tikka, skewered marinated lamb and many other things: salads, and more. Very flavoursome and really quite rich too.

 For 2–4   5 minutes   50 minutes

3–4 good size beetroot, scrubbed and halved

2–3 garlic cloves

3–4 tablespoons of olive oil

1 teaspoon of ground cumin

1/2 tsp ground coriander

150g full fat live yoghurt

Roast the beetroot on a tray for 45 minutes at 160–170°C.
    Then put all the ingredients in a blender. Season a little with salt and pepper.

Serve with flatbreads or similar as a starter, or with salads and more as a side to a main. This is best when the cumin and coriander are freshly toasted and ground. It makes for a really powerful and tasty dish.

MY LOCKDOWN COOKBOOK

Braised Tomatoes, Chick Peas and Spinach

More an easy and healthy supper than a side; could be a lunch too. Serve with flatbreads or rice, and maybe a samosa on the side or something similar.

For 2   10 minutes   50 minutes

1/2 tsp roasted and ground cumin seeds

2 to 3 cloves of garlic, crushed and chopped

1 medium onion or 2 small shallots finely chopped

1 large red chilli de-seeded

2 tsp tomato paste

1 large cup dried chickpeas, soaked overnight then simmered for 2 hours (or a 400g can)

60–70g pitted olives

250–300g big beef tomatoes cut into chunks

150g spinach

2 tsp wine vinegar

Salt and pepper

Pour some oil into a pot and add the garlic and onion, fry gently till soft. Then add the cumin and finely chopped chilli and some salt and pepper. Continue frying gently for another few minutes.

Add the tomato paste, chickpeas and olives, and some water to just about cover, then simmer away for a good 30 minutes, stirring occasionally.

Place the tomato chunks on top of it all, spread out evenly so they cover it, and then do the same with the spinach. Turn the heat up a little and allow it to cook till the spinach wilts down.

Add the 2 teaspoons of red or white wine vinegar and mix it all carefully so it does not break the tomato chunks.

European and North American Dishes

In the way that other world cuisines developed and were influenced by such things as weather, religion and conflict, so did ours. Our climate is temperate; we get a good mix of seasons and temperatures, and with that comes rain, wind and sun, and occasionally snow too. So summer salads and new potatoes and winter stews and roasts. That's the simple view!

Back in the 18th and 19th centuries, our cuisine in the UK was as broad and full as that of the other European nations such as France and Italy. But the world wars of the 20th century ravaged our nation, and that included what we eat. Two world wars meant that, from the second decade right through to the 1950s, our culture was shredded. Food supplies were rationed and restaurants struggled; black markets in things like sausages and eggs sprang up, too. This meant that two generations of families suffered, and as a result they lost the knowledge, experience and richness of our culture and cuisine. So when I was a boy in the 1950s, my parents still had ration cards. When things like butter and cream, and sugar and spices returned, it was such a treat for them. So for my parents, and their parents before them, food was not the joy it once was and has become once again for us. I remember going fishing in the Norfolk rivers and sea with Dad and joining the villagers in the fields at harvest time to club rabbit and hare as they were cornered by the combine harvesters in the fields. Mum would take us to gather fruit from the hedgerows: blackberries and damsons for pie, crumbles and jam, and elderberries for wine. In September, Dad would wake me and my brother as the sun was rising to beat the locals to the fields to pick huge mushrooms the size of plates. It was what everyone did to broaden their diet and to save money.

The introduction of the fridge changed the lives of everyone. Before these were commonplace in people's homes, it was difficult to keep things fresh; it was a struggle to stop produce going off, so meat was cooked to death and vegetables were so well cooked they offered no resistance to a knife or fork!

So as I grew up, things improved, and Dad grew stuff at home too. Eventually I left home and went to study for a degree in London. My eyes and taste buds were opened there and I had my first Chinese meal and my first curry. So much has changed; today we can buy food from all over the world, which although not so good for the planet has made it possible to cook almost any cuisine at home.

What follows is a selection of foods that I like to eat regularly. Not the meat and three veg I was brought up with, but a varied selection.

A Basic Beef Stew

This was cooked by my mum when I was at home, so an awfully long while ago! At the time, beef was cheap compared to chicken so it was the more everyday meat.

This dish has so little in it, just beef and carrot, that the seasoning and the pressure cooking are the key to its flavour. I'm not really sure how it would turn out if cooked in a saucepan or casserole, or for how long. However, this is so very easy once you have a pressure cooker.

A pressure cooker just saves time for almost any dish that needs hours. Chilli con carne is excellent in a pressure cooker; chorizo and beans, too. (I will get to those later.)

For 2   10 minutes   1 hour

300–400g braising steak	2–3 bay leaves
2–3 largish organic or 'heritage' carrots	1 tablespoon plain flour
	Red wine if available
Ground salt and pepper	Splash of olive oil or chunk of butter

Dice the beef and remove the stringy stuff. Mix in the flour.

Put the pressure cooker on to the heat and put the oil or butter in. When it's hot, add the beef and fry. Stir regularly; otherwise, the beef will stick to the bottom and sides.

When the meat is all browned, chuck in the carrots in big bite-size chunks and then add salt and pepper and stir for a minute or so.

Cover with boiling water, add the bay leaves, and a good slosh of red wine if you have some handy (if not, it's optional). Scrape around the side and bottom to remove the burnt stuff, as this will add to the colour and help the final sauce. Put the lid on and turn the heat up so the pressure cooker builds up pressure.

Once it's gently hissing away, turn the heat down. Cook for 45 minutes, then turn off. (Do not try to open yet!)

After 10 minutes or so the cooker should be ready to open. Inside it should still have plenty of liquid, so now, with the lid off, scrape the sides where it's still sticky and simmer till reduced so the juices are colourful. Taste to judge consistency and add seasoning.

Serve with mash, or potatoes of your choice and some fresh veg.

A Basic Tomato Sauce

This is the easy place to start. A basic tomato sauce goes with pasta for a simple veggie quick dish, and chicken, fish or a schnitzel.

For 2 — **1 hour**

A large shallot or medium size onion, chopped

3 garlic cloves, crushed

olive oil

A standard (400g) tin of chopped tomatoes

2 bay leaves

oregano

fresh basil, chopped

Parmesan, grated

salt and black pepper

Take a large shallot or medium size onion and chop finely. Crush 3 garlic cloves. Pour some olive oil into a saucepan, fry the onions and garlic gently till they're really soft.

Add a tin of chopped tomatoes, grind in a little salt and a generous quantity of black pepper, 2 bay leaves and a generous quantity of oregano. Bring to the boil, then put the lid on and simmer for an hour. Stir occasionally, if it's starting to stick add water.

If you have some, chop fresh basil and add it at the end. Boil some pasta, mix this in, grate Parmesan over it and enjoy!

This sauce works in many ways: pour over a chicken leg that's roasted; fry a schnitzel and have this on the side mixed into pasta. So many ways this simple sauce works. Boil some stuffed pasta and stir this sauce in before serving. Toast an old baguette and spread it on top. Use your imagination! Don't forget, the fresh oregano and basil make a real difference, so get some pots for the windowsill and start growing!

For a lovely sauce with fish, add a cup full of chopped black olives with the tin of tomatoes at the beginning, and this will simmer for 60–90 minutes. For a richer fuller flavour, add some Malbec or other robust red wine. Again, chop some fresh basil in at the end.

We are currently addicted to meat balls with this sauce. You can buy 20 meatballs for £3 from the supermarket or make them from minced beef with a little seasoning. Fry the meatballs on all sides, starting with a dry pan, then once the sauce has come to the boil, add the fried browned meatballs. Simmer for at least 2 hours. I usually turn it off after 2 hours, rest it for an hour then cook again, depending on time available. Again, if there's a bottle of red around, pour some in at the beginning and again, if you have some fresh basil chuck it in near the end.

Stuffed pasta with tomato sauce and basil

Cooking with Wine

Coq au vin and boeuf bourguignon come to mind? Lamb shank in a red wine sauce? They are probably the most well known, but they are still just the tip of quite an iceberg. They are all best cooked in a lidded casserole dish in the oven and they all have similar ingredients.

Coq au vin

In fact, you could start any of these by browning the meat and setting it aside and then putting a few shallots and garlic cloves in to fry in the juices, maybe adding a bit more oil and then slowly adding in red wine (a good Malbec or Claret would be best). Some people like to add a handful of chestnut mushrooms at some point, more often towards the end of the cooking time. Once you have the wine seasoned with salt pepper and bay leaves, you add back the meat – be sure there is enough wine to partly cover the meat – and put the lid on. Pop it in the oven at a mid temperature, 140/150°C or so, for at least 90 minutes, if not two hours – especially with the beef, as a cheaper cut of steak is always best for flavour but needs time to soften. When this is done, the wine should be reduced to a rich gravy – you can thicken it with arrowroot, for example; I prefer it as it is – and can be served with potato and veg in your chosen style.

MY LOCKDOWN COOKBOOK

Cooking with wine is a way of enriching the flavours of your dish. Generally, white wine is used with fish and chicken dishes – although, of course, our coq au vin is with red. It's something that can be added to many things: a Bolognese sauce, for example, benefits, as do many casseroles and sauces.

There are many variations on the theme of cooking with white wine and cream too, sometimes with the addition of mustard. Essentially, if it's for fish, the sauce is made first by frying onion and garlic with herbs and seasoning and then adding the wine and then some cream till you have a lovely creamy sauce to which the fish is added to cook for a matter of minutes. The chicken version, on the other hand, would again be started with the onion and garlic, but then you would add the chicken before the wine and cream so that the chicken gets plenty of time to cook and soften a little.

There are many ways with red or white wine: they all enrich the dish and produce a sauce fuller in flavour. Parsley or thyme seem to be commonly used in these dishes, and sometimes marjoram. I have made my own versions of these dishes depending upon what's in the fridge. It's fun to experiment, and as long as you remember the basics of how long the meat or fish needs to cook, you will not go far wrong. Fish is delicate and can be over-seasoned, whilst beef or lamb can be more robust.

For Moules marinière, a very popular seafood dish, fry a generous quantity of garlic and then add a little white wine and a little thickener. Keep adding wine and stirring till you have quite a good quantity, chuck in the mussels and add some chopped parsley and simmer for 15–20 minutes. Delicious!

Spaghetti Bolognese

10 minutes   2-4 hours

Really? But everyone knows how to make that! That's probably true. But I like to think we are all open to suggestions and changes. There are in truth many so-called authentic recipes. Look online and you will see what I mean. Different regions of Italy and even different cities make the claim that theirs is best or is the original. In Italy, they argue over this in the same way that they argue over whose pizza reigns supreme. Most of us here in the UK think 'spag bol' is made with minced beef, yet if you have already looked into this you will have noticed that quite a number of Italian recipes have pork or a mixture of meats. The point, it seems to me, is not just what meat you use, but how long it's cooked for and how much of the fat you include. Then there are the herbs: oregano or basil, thyme or bay leaves. Not to mention the vegetables: some say carrot, celery or sometimes mushrooms, and the arguments rage.

So, this is my easy way. If it's an everyday meal, I just buy one pack of minced beef – organic is best – always at least 10% fat. The meat is the main ingredient, so the better the meat then the better the flavour. If I want to make more for any reason – like having guests or wanting to freeze some – I will often buy a pack of pork.

First, always cook the meat so the fat comes out: be sure to brown it all. Then you can add the finely chopped onion and crushed garlic, which will fry in the meat's fat. Be sure to do this on quite a high heat, so any moisture in the meat is boiled off and the onion and garlic is fried, not boiled!

Then it's time to add a can or more of tomatoes, and some tomato paste. For me, for every pack of meat, it's a can of tomatoes. If I add another pack of mince, then often I add a quarter to a third of a tube of tomato paste or the second tin. At this point, too, I will grind in salt and black pepper and quite a good quantity of fresh oregano, and two big bay leaves or a few smaller ones. Ideally, this will bubble away on the lowest heat with the lid on for an hour or so, at which point I like a cup of red wine added in. This will then simmer away, occasionally stirred, for another couple of hours at least; occasionally a little water will be needed.

In my experience, it's good to turn it off and leave it for a few hours or even till the next day. But for it to be ready to eat, all the ingredients must have cooked down: the tomatoes and onion and herbs are all 'gone' or cooked into the sauce; it's rich and not at all watery. I would say, it's almost impossible to overcook this but easy not to cook it enough. It's a lovely rich sauce that has depth of flavour, even without the red wine. Cooked for hours, it's lovely.

As for time, minimum of two hours. Best of all the next day after quite a few hours of cooking. It really is a personal thing and down to how much time you can devote to it. However, it gets better the longer it's cooked, for sure!

Chilli Con Carne

So many ways to make this! The quantity of chilli just depends on your taste buds. This is my version. I always make a good sized potful, as it freezes so well and can be saved for another, more hurried day.

For four people or more, this will take quite a while! The longer it cooks the better: minimum two hours. This is one of those dishes that work really well in a pressure cooker, as one hour in the cooker is the same as three-plus hours on the hob.

For 4   **2 hours (at least)**

700–800g of minced beef, not the low fat but 10% or more.

2 tins of kidney beans (or 250–300g of dried beans, soaked for 24 hours)

2 large onions

A lot of garlic

Chilli flakes to taste

About a third of a tomato paste tube.

2 well heaped teaspoons of cumin

1 teaspoon of paprika

A generous quantity of thyme

A few bay leaves

2 large squares of dark chocolate

A generous quantity of sea salt and black pepper

Take a large saucepan or a pressure cooker. Drop all the minced beef in and fry on high heat. Stir and stir.

When it's all brown – not red – add the finely chopped onion and the crushed garlic and continue frying and stirring. This takes time, as the onion should be frying in the fat from the beef.

Add the spice, salt and pepper and chill and keep stirring. When it's fragrant, add the tomato paste. Keep stirring.

When it's all well mixed, cooked and fragrant, add the beans. Stir well.

Finally, add some boiling water and the herbs. If you're using a saucepan, use enough water so that it's just covering, but if it's a pressure cooker the water should be at least an inch over the ingredients.

Pressure cook for 90 minutes and then simmer to get the right consistency. For the saucepan it's really a low heat with some stirring and occasionally adding water, for as long as you can manage. I often do this for 4+ hours and leave it till the next day and cook again. For either, when it's really cooked well, simmering away, quite thick, add the chocolate and cook for another 10 minutes, stirring it in well.

I love it with basmati rice, mashed avocado and soured cream or creamy yoghurt.

Red Cabbage

Somehow this only really works with duck, sausages or Christmas turkey. But it's perfect with them. It's the fatty nature of the duck and rich turkey dinner that's offset somehow by the slightly tart cabbage. (Sprouts do the same, I think, but nothing like as tasty, in my view!)

For 4   **5 minutes**   **1 hour 15 minutes +**

1 whole red cabbage

2 cooking apples

5–6 cloves

1/2 -3/4 tsp cream of tartar

2–3 teaspoons sugar

1 tbsp olive oil

Halve then quarter the cabbage. Then carefully remove the central tough stalk. Chop into inch by half inch pieces. Peal and core the apples and slice into small thin pieces.

Put the oil in a good size saucepan and on low to medium heat, add all the cabbage and turn and stir well for quite a few minutes. This helps soften the cabbage which is quite crisp and thick.

Add the apples, sugar, cream of tartar and cloves, and half a cup or so of water. Stir it all thoroughly, being sure it's well mixed.

Then just simmer with the lid on for 45–60 minutes, stirring regularly. The apple should have disappeared; if not, simmer and stir till it has.

Turn the heat off and let it stand for a while. If it gets cold that's OK too: re-heat thoroughly and simmer for another 15 minutes before serving.

Be sure to keep it moist, but you do not want any liquid at the bottom when it's done. Do not let the cabbage reduce to a mush: it's overdone then.

Caramelised Red Onion Quiche

We have eaten this so many times now. The sausage rolls that come later are amazing; this is not far short of those. Truly tasty and healthy. You need a deep 18cm fluted tin with a removable base, then it's all going to fit in and will serve easily too.

　　　　　　　　　　　　　　　MY LOCKDOWN COOKBOOK

 For 2 30 minutes 30/35 minutes

Short crust pastry in a block, rolled quite thinly, or homemade.

Plain flour for dusting

1 large red onion

2 large or 3 medium eggs

Extra mature crumbly cheddar

A small pot of double cream.

Roll out the pastry so it's quite thin: less than half a centimetre. Bake the pastry blind till it's beginning to brown: this takes about 20 minutes at 200°C.

While that's going on, caramelise the onions: finely slice them, add to melted butter in a frying pan, stir them about so they are all coated in butter, and soften them. Then, sprinkle about a teaspoon of white sugar over the onions, stir it in and then fry gently, stirring every so often. Takes about 15 minutes to caramelise. So, ready at the same time as the pastry, roughly, though it's important that the pastry is cooked first, so you can chop the cheddar into small bits, spread it across the bottom and spread the onion over that straight from the pan, still hot!

Then beat the eggs well, add at least half the pot of cream and beat again so it's still frothy. Pour over the cheese and onion. Put it straight back into the oven at 200°C and keep an eye on it. After about 20 or 25 minutes, it should have risen to almost double its height and be a mid-brown tone on top. That's it.

Carefully remove the fluted side, leaving the quiche on the metal tray to put on the table. We eat half each, greedily.

Love this in the summer with warm potato salad and spring onions, chives and mayo mixed in, or plain with mayo, or just melted butter, crispy salad leaves and tomato salad with lots of fresh basil, and home-made coleslaw. In the winter it's a baked potato and greens, or maybe salad if nice fresh leaves are available. Yummy.

Chorizo and Beans

This dish derives from an American pork and bean dish that I tried to make. It cooked for hours and stuck to the bottom, so I gave up on it. Years later, when I had a pressure cooker, I decided to try the dish again. This time it worked and was very nice. Then, I decided to replace the pork with chorizo and changed all the seasoning. Now it's a big favourite. Love it. So easy too.

For 2 | **10 minutes** | **1 hour 10 minutes**

1 stick of chorizo (Lidl does a lovely one for less than 2 quid)

About 125g of dry cannellini beans, soaked in a bowl for about 24 hours.

1 big shallot

Generous handful of fresh parsley

Similar quantity of fresh oregano (if dried, at least a heaped teaspoon, I would guess)

2 bay leaves

A generous squeeze of tomato paste

More ground black pepper than you'd think

Just a little salt.

In the pressure cooker, pour in a generous quantity of olive oil. Add the finely chopped shallot and fry till it begins to brown.

Add the chorizo, sliced and then halved so it's about half an inch thick – don't forget to remove the skin, though! Stir continuously till the chorizo starts to release its coloured oil. Add the tomato paste, and then the herbs and stir well.

Add the salt and pepper. Once it's all mixed well and is hot and steamy, pour the bowl of beans through a sieve, removing all the water, and add to the mix. Pour in boiling water to cover, plus half an inch at least.

Put the lid on and pressure cook for 45 minutes. Then turn it off, wait till it's ready to open, then turn on the heat to reduce, stir regularly, till its no longer watery, then it's done.

This sauce turns thicker the cooler it gets, so do not reduce it too much.

Best with freshly baked baguette, griddled courgettes, greens or your choice. Alternatively, experiment widely!

Chipotle Pork Chops

A regular favourite here now: one quarter of a tasty and healthy meal that's easy to cook.

MY LOCKDOWN COOKBOOK

For 2

 5 minutes + marinade time   **10/12 minutes**

2 boneless pork chops, fat on, no more than half an inch thick.

Chipotle sauce (so many versions of this available: experiment away!)

1/2 a fresh lime

Ordinary honey

For the wedges:

Sweet potatoes

Olive oil

paprika

cayenne

Put the chops on a board. With a sharp knife, cut through the fat on the edge at every inch or so. Then score shallowly, both sides in a crisis cross pattern. Then put them in a food bag with plenty of space, squeeze the lime and pour the juice in; take 2–3 heaped teaspoons of chipotle paste and pour that in, and then a good teaspoon of honey too. Tie the bag up so its sealed and massage it thoroughly so all of it is mixed up and covering the meat – don't be too firm, though, or either the meat or the bag will split!

Put the marinaded chops in the fridge – all day, if you can. You can gently massage them a few times; if not, they will still be fine.

Grill the chops, turning regularly, adding sauce from the bag if it gets dry at all. The fat will blacken due to the honey. All in all, the grilling takes 8–10 minutes.

Serve with sweet potato wedges. Make these by peeling sweet potatoes, then cutting to wedges; put in another plastic bag, tip a little olive oil in, then a teaspoon or so paprika and a sprinkling of cayenne, massage well. Tip onto an oven tray and bake for 30–35 minutes.

Serve with homemade coleslaw and a tomato salad. Lovely combination!

My Easy Sauerkraut

This is not like it is in the bought jars. It's more crunchy and crisp. It's similar to the kind found in many German restaurants that are not fancy and make large batches that are served in a few days at most. It's really nice with sausages, and anything else you want to try it with. Great for the tummy, too.

1 large cabbage – not a frilly one, just the round solid type.

1 large organic carrot.

1 tablespoon of Caraway seeds

You need a big bowl into which you put your finely shredded cabbage and the carrot. The real process is to beat the crap out of it. There are many ways to do this. I use the mortar from my pestle and take probably a half an hour to bash it about. Remember, if you are using a bowl it's almost certainly glass or similar so you mustn't hit it hard. It does work if you put the ingredients in a large freezer bag and strike it with a rolling pin! Some people prefer to massage it between their hands.

Whichever method you use, do not hurry: this is really all there is to do, and you can tell when you have done enough as the veg noticeably starts to give out liquid. You will see a few millimetres of liquid at the bottom of the bowl, especially if it's a glass one. When the liquid appears, you can pour in the caraway seeds: 1 tablespoon is a minimum; I use nearer 2 as it's such a good flavour. Stir it well.

So sterilise a big jar or a few small ones and, without touching the inside of jar or lid, spoon the mixture in. Once you get to half full, press it down with the back of your spoon. Then keep spooning it in and pressing it down. Leave an inch at least of space between it and the lid, as it should ferment and expand a little.

Fit the lids tightly and put in a dark cupboard for a couple or three days at most to ferment and then transfer to the fridge. If you make it in summer when it's hot, 24 hours in a cupboard should be long enough.

It will last weeks in the fridge with a tightly fitting lid.

Pork and Prunes

No idea where this came from. I have been cooking it for so long. Might be from a Spanish cookbook I lent out decades ago and never saw again. Strange thing, that! Lending books seems to end that way so often.

Shoulder is the only cut that really works, as the fatty nature helps to make a rich sauce that's essential for this dish. The dramatic part, flambé, really adds a depth of flavour here, although I have to confess the dish is still good without it.

I have always used a medium-sized frying pan with a heavy base and a well-fitting lid to make this dish.

For 2   10 minutes   1 hour 40 minutes

300–400g of pork shoulder

1 large onion or 2 good shallots

3–4 garlic cloves

Ground sea salt and black pepper

Good handful of semi-dried prunes

2–3 bay leaves

Handful of fresh parsley

Large dollop of cooking brandy Armagnac or calvados (cheap stuff is fine)

Large splash of oil

Pour in some olive oil or melt some butter. When it's hot but not smoky, add the finely chopped onion and crushed garlic.

Stir away till the onion and garlic are translucent but not browning around the edges, then add the pork, chopped into generous bite-size pieces. Stir away, being sure to brown not boil the meat.

When it's looking good, partly or wholly browned but not crisped at all, throw in your alcohol, about half a cup, then carefully set light to the dish. If you use gas, it's easy, with the flame on high, just tilt the pan and the dish will ignite in the flame. Using electricity, you will need to light it yourself. So, whatever way, keep your hair and head back, turn on your extractor to full and stand back while lighting it with extended hands. Dramatic! The flames soon subside.

Turn the heat down and the extractor too. Now add all the salt, pepper and herbs, then cover with boiling water and add the prunes. Bring to the boil, then immediately drop the lid on and be sure it's a good fit.

Leave for a while and stir gently occasionally, to make sure it does not stick or reduce too much. You are better off adding a bit of water if you think it's getting too reduced.

After 2 hours of this, the whole thing should be dark in colour, the pork soft and the prunes almost sludgy; the gravy should not be too thick nor watery. Hmm, hard to describe further, use your judgement! It's done.

I like to serve this with crisped baked potatoes that soak up the tasty juices, and whatever fresh veg is in the fridge. Hearty greens always my choice. Boiled or steamed, as the dish itself is fully flavoured – no need for further complexity.

Spinach Soufflé

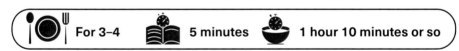 For 3–4   5 minutes   1 hour 10 minutes or so

50g of butter

50g of plain flour

Lots of fresh milk

4 good sized eggs

French mustard

At least 100g mature crumbly cheddar

A bag of spinach

Take a good-sized soufflé dish, 17–18 cm across and quite deep, 10cm at least, and grease then flour it all round inside. Melt the butter in a large saucepan and slowly add the flour over a low heat, stirring it in so eventually it's all a mushy mix. This is like a classic white sauce.

So, after frying for a few minutes, slowly add the milk, stirring over the low heat, bit by bit so it does not go lumpy. After about 10 minutes you should have a smooth paste-like mix. Now add some mustard: the more you add the more the heat. Finely grate the cheese and stir this all in, adding some salt and pepper. When this is all mixed and the cheese has melted in, turn off the heat.

      MY LOCKDOWN COOKBOOK

Now, separate the yolks from the whites, beat the yolks – they do not change texture much, just make it creamier – and mix in, then beat the whites thoroughly, till they are peaked, and fold this all in gently. Finally, add finely shredded/chopped fresh spinach: remove the stalks and discard first, then when it's truly shredded into thin short strips, mix this in too. Be careful: the beaten eggs need to keep the airiness, so be gentle.

Now, take the mix and gently pour it in to the soufflé dish. Put it in the fan oven at about 190–200°C and wait and watch! When it has risen and lightly brown on top it's done. As for the timing, it should take around 25–30 minutes. Never the same twice, unless you measure everything – which I never do. Another test of being ready is that when it's risen, it should still be just a little wobbly; if you take it out of the oven too soon, it will sink and sag.

If you fancy individual ones, use four ramekins and cook for 10–15 minutes.

For chocolate soufflé, no cheese or mustard, replace half the flour with cocoa powder. You can make a creamy chocolate sauce to pour over or around these. Very tasty, and not scary!

Follow the instructions to begin with, then you can start changing things. Try flaked salmon instead of spinach? But anything heavy, like red meat, will sink to the bottom. Be adventurous.

I like to have a soufflé with baked potato and melted butter with greens or salad.

Steak and Mushroom Pie

Not a Sunday roast! But great on Sunday.

This I meant to learn to cook for a long while. It's made up to be the way I think a good rich pie should be. So it takes time for it to cook, to get the sauce rich and the meat soft.

For 2   10 minutes   2 hours 15 minutes

400g of braising steak

250g of chestnut mushrooms

1 large onion or 2 good shallots

2–3 garlic cloves

2–3 bay leaves

1 half teaspoon of fresh thyme

Quite a lot of good red wine: a Malbec or something similarly robust

Ground salt and pepper

½ tablespoon of cornflour (optional)

1 pack of all butter ready-made puff pastry in a roll (or in a slab, which you then roll to about 15mm or just over half an inch)

Finely chop the onions and crush the garlic. Tip some oil or melt some butter into a saucepan and gently fry the onion and garlic.

Meanwhile, you can remove the stringy bits from the meat, leaving the fat on. Cut it into bite-size pieces. Spread it on a board – or better, in a food bag – and add the cornflour and mix well. Then add to the onions and turn up the heat. The meat will stick, the pan will brown around the edges.

Keep stirring for 6–8 minutes till it's browned and pour in wine to cover it, then add the salt, pepper and herbs. Bring to the boil, then turn it down to just simmering. Stir occasionally, adding water occasionally if it gets too thick, and cook like this for at least 90 minutes and up to 2 hours.

Then, chop the mushrooms into quarters and add them in, adding more liquid if necessary.

After a further 15 minutes, pour it all into an 18cm across deep pie dish: it should come to within an inch or 3 centimetres of the top. Place a prop like an egg cup upside down in the middle of the dish. Then, just take the roll of pastry and place it over the whole dish. Press the pastry with a fork onto the edge of the dish, all round. Then carefully cut all the spare off. Carefully cut a slit into the middle so the steam is released while it cooks. Then brush with melted butter or, even better, beaten egg.

Place the pie in the oven on an oven tray at 190°C and make sure there is plenty of room for the pastry to rise. Putting it on a tray catches the juice so you only have to clean the tray rather than the oven! Cook for 40 minutes or so, till the pastry has risen and browned and crisp.

I like this with baked potatoes and tenderstem broccoli. It's a bit of a performance, but really worth it if you like a good pie.

Salmon and Cod Fishcakes

For starters or mains. This should make six to eight cakes, depending upon size. So gauging time is difficult; suffice it to say, a bit of practice brings you to about one hour comfortably.

Ingredients can be varied to suit what's available and your personal taste. Clearly, it's best to start roughly with this recipe, then you will know what, if anything, to change!

6–8 fishcakes

30 minutes + fridge time · **15 minutes**

200/225g salmon, skin and bone removed

300/325g cod or similar white fish, no skin or bone

400+g boiled potato

2 large eggs, well beaten

Zest of half a lemon

Handful of chopped parsley

Squeeze of tomato paste

Breadcrumbs

Cook the fish and flake it well. In a bowl, mix the ingredients together thoroughly and season well. Take an oven tray or board and cover lightly with flour.

Try to judge and take an eighth of the mix and slowly form into a ball, rolling gently between your palms. Takes a bit of practice, and if at first you don't succeed…! Then, when it's a sticky ball, flatten it gently to a thick 1½-inch thick disk.

Take two bowls and put the beaten eggs in one and the breadcrumbs in the other. Take the first cake and pass it through the egg, making sure it's well covered, and then place in the breadcrumbs and turn it gently till it's well covered. Repeat for each cake, placing them on a tray which then goes in the fridge to set.

After an hour or so they are ready to fry, gently. They will need at least 8–10 minutes per side until the breadcrumbs have browned.

It's okay to just flour the cakes gently on a board and not do the whole breadcrumb thing. The cakes are not so firmly formed, however, and greater care is needed when handling them. Your choice! I advise trying the breadcrumb way first.

Lovely with crisp salads, freshly baked bread…

Jerk Chicken, Pork or Fish

This has become very popular. Dunn's River brand is a good Jamaican sauce. However, like other brands, it can be really hot. They do sell different versions with 1 to 2 or 3 chillies on the label. I find so often it's the hot one that's available, so I recommend adding other stuff to the sauce.

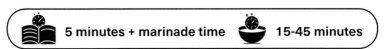

5 minutes + marinade time   15-45 minutes

For me and most people I have served this to, I mix one third – or a half if they are OK with hot food – of the jerk sauce with measures of tomato ketchup, brown sauce, BBQ sauce, hoisin sauce, tonkatsu sauce and so on. Make it up as you go along. It's the jerk flavour that will dominate, so do not use strong flavoured sauces like oyster sauce, as it will conflict and be odd.

Chicken – with a sharp knife, deeply slash a leg or two thighs per person and then pop them in a bag and pour in the sauce and massage well. The longer you leave it the better. 45 minutes in the oven at 190°C

Pork – boneless chops, belly without skin or shoulder. With these cuts, add some lime or lemon juice so the meat is tenderised and a little honey so the fatty bits crisp up. Best grilled or in a fan oven, turned regularly. Overcook if you are concerned, but these pork cuts cook through quite quickly.

Fish – use firm fish like swordfish, huss, salmon or monkfish. Add the lime juice but no honey. In a fan oven, a salmon steak will take 12–15 minutes as a guide at 190°C.

All these are lovely with brown rice, coleslaw and tomato salad. Potato wedges are OK too, but I would do the paprika and cayenne mixed in a bag treatment. Sweet potatoes are also really good.

I can eat this every week, really!

Sun-Dried Tomato Risotto

I have always loved this. It's creamy, full of flavour, and although it requires constant attention, it's not a long haul.

For 3–4 | 10 minutes | 30/35 minutes

250g risotto rice (Arborio is best, I find)

1 large onion

2–3 garlic cloves

A large pot of chicken stock

At least a cup full of sundried tomatoes.

Parmesan to grate

Single cream

A big chunk of butter

Salt and pepper

This method is not difficult, easy to follow and easy to adapt. But each step is important and needs to be followed… So no short cuts!

Finely chop the onion and crush the garlic, add a chunk of butter, about an ounce, to 24–25cm diameter frying pan. Gently fry till soft, then pour all the rice in and stir it to coat it and mix it. After a couple of minutes it should all be hot and beginning to dry.

So, pour in some chicken stock and cover the contents. On a lowish heat, let it bubble away till it's all absorbed. At this point, set a timer for 25 minutes.

Now add the sun-dried tomatoes, all chopped up, and grind in sea salt and pepper and stir again. Add enough stock to cover again and now simmer.

Keep this process of adding stock and simmering going for 20 of the 25 minutes. Do not let it dry and do not add too much. Then, at about the 20-minute mark, you need to add enough stock such that in a few more minutes it's not very wet and not very dry!

Hmmm – this is where you will learn by experience. No matter, though. At about the 25-minute mark, grate a good pile of Parmesan and mix it in and then add some single cream and mix that in too. In order to be ready to serve – and you can add more tomatoes at this point or you could add chopped mushrooms at the 20-minute point – the risotto should be sticky and creamy, red-coloured from the tomatoes too. If it's still sloppy, leave it to reduce for a few minutes more. It will not spoil. The important thing is to get it thick, sticky and creamy.

I love to eat this with griddled baby courgette and a small pile of queen scallops. A bit expensive, maybe? That's just my favourite combination. You can eat this with whatever takes your fancy. Enjoy!

The Best Ever Sausage Rolls

This was found in a Sunday paper top 10 cookery list, along with the earlier quiche. They are utterly lovely. Truly the best ever! Simplified, as always.

For 4

15 minutes + fridge time   40 minutes

500g minced pork

125g unsmoked streaky bacon

1 good size shallot

2 tablespoons brown sauce

Fresh thyme, a good heaped cupful

Fresh parsley, another good heaped cupful

3–4 cloves of garlic

Level teaspoon nutmeg

Salt and pepper

1 roll all-butter puff pastry

Egg to glaze

Finely chop or crush all the ingredients and put them and the minced pork, the finely chopped bacon and everything else in a large bowl and mix it all up thoroughly.

Take the pastry roll and roll it out on a floured surface. Tip the mixture onto it, then arrange it as a long even pile one third of the way across, with the pastry length ways and the mix along that. Then take the long two-thirds left and fold/roll it over so you have a couple of inches of doubled up pastry and the mix nicely surrounded and as round as you can get it – be gentle with the pastry, so you do not make any holes or splits. (If you do, re-roll the pastry, turning it on itself a number of times so the hole or split is rolled away.)

Take a fork, and press the spare 2 inches or so together all along it, so the roll is tightly contained. Now, take a sharp knife and cut it in two.

Take an oven tray, cover it in greaseproof paper, and carefully place the 2 pieces apart on the tray. Cover it and put it in the fridge to set for an hour or so.

Take it out, and with a sharp knife, score the top at an angle all along. Beat your egg yolk, brush carefully all over, grind salt over the top and sprinkle with thyme leaves. Cut each large piece into 4 or 5 equal pieces. Space them out evenly so you have at least an inch between the pieces.

Put it in the oven at 190°C for 30 minutes and a finish at 170°C for another 10 minutes. It should be brown and crisp, and smell very appetising.

Rest on the tray for 5 minutes before serving. Lovely with salads and all sorts of things as a main meal or home-made spicy tomato sauce or mustard. Really lovely! Make it for friends and watch their surprise!

Salads

Salads are a big part of meals at home all year round and very simple and quick to make, and healthy once you know how.

Tomato and Onion

Tomatoes are everywhere; fresh and local are best. Start with a small serving bowl, chop the tomatoes into the bowl, then grind salt in and mix with a gurgle of olive oil. Add halved, thinly sliced red onion and mix, then add a little balsamic or red wine vinegar. Excellent with shredded fresh basil leaves.

Coleslaw

Organic carrots are cheap and the best. Any crisp cabbage will work; start with white round ones. Peel and grate a large carrot and put in a medium-size serving bowl, carve off a segment of the cabbage equal to 3 times the size of your carrot – roughly! Shred or slice finely with a sharp knife. Mix well, add about 1½ tbsp of mayonnaise and mix well. Lovely and fresh.

Beetroot Salad

Very simple and very healthy. Take 1 large or 2 medium beets and scrub the skin, then grate into a serving bowl. Then peel and top a good size carrot and grate that in too. Mix well and add half a tablespoon of red wine or balsamic vinegar and a tablespoon of olive oil.

Greek Salad

Finely chopped or crumbled feta cheese, chopped tomatoes, finely sliced and halved cucumber, chopped/sliced red onion, all dressed with equal oil and red wine vinegar.

Potato Salad

Made with boiled then chopped and cooled new potatoes mixed with finely chopped spring onion and mayo.

So many more combinations of fresh leaves and vegetables. Consult the web and find more. Rocket is really tasty and great as a garnish and as a food. Lots of varieties of lettuce to make all sorts. Caesar salad, Niçoise and many more.

Cakes and Puddings

My downfall! As far back as I can remember, my mum used to bake things that were a treat. In those days, the cakes, pies and puddings were neither complicated nor exotic. They were simple, and the recipes passed from one generation to the next. I was brought up with shortbread, Victoria sponges, fruit cake and buns, apple pie and blackberry crumble. Some of these I make myself and some I have rarely made; some you will find in this book.

Cakes these days are indulgent. I have to be very strict with myself as I can be a real piggy. I adore cake and I am addicted to sugar. Knowing this helps, and I can be sure that cake is a treat and not an everyday thing. I have the luxury of a good size garden so I can indulge in bowls of strawberries and raspberries with no fear, and soon my all-time summer favourite, the Victoria plum, will be hanging off the trees I planted a few years ago. My mum would make delicious pies, tarts and crumbles during the summer with these delicious fruits. Then, every year she would make the jams that took us through the winter so we had something to spread on our toast. Mum could pour generous quantities of jam into a pastry base for the best Bakewell tarts.

I hope you enjoy some of the lovely and still quite easy and simple recipes for truly indulgent home baking.

The one thing to remember is the nature of our ovens! If I set my oven to 200°C it will be different to yours – not by much maybe, but still it means that you will need to be flexible about the precise temperature. I know this all too well, having moved house quite a few times over the years. Although I have usually bought the basic Bosch double oven that fits under the worktop, each time it's been the same experience: readjusting to the exact nature of the oven. Currently, many things cook well at 200°C, but it's noticeable that if you turn the temperature up by just a little, it can make a much bigger difference than it should. So failures are often not your fault and are to be expected. If a cake is gooey inside but cooked on top, that means the oven was too hot. If the cake rises well and is cooked thoroughly but a little dry, then again it's overcooked, but this time by time. If in doubt, as ever consult the web with simple questions, and the answers come easily.

Apricot Tart and Bakewell Tart

Bakewell tart

Both quite similar in the way they are made, and both truly irresistible for me. The Bakewell is a true English tradition, whilst the apricot tart more of a recent pleasure.

So, I would say I make these tarts for guests, and it depends upon how many as to how big. I have a 7-inch tin, which has 4 portions – no seconds! Then there's a 9½ inch which is good for 6–8 comfortably, and finally an 11½ inch which is good for 10–12. These are tins with a removable base and fluted sides. The Bakewell tin should be 4cm+ deep, whereas the apricot tart tin need only be 3cm or so. Buy or make sweet shortcrust pastry for your choice of tin and bake blind. For this recipe, use the mid-size tin.

For 8   1 hour

1 hour/1 hour 15 minutes (Bakewell)

25/30 minutes (Apricot)

Pastry:

50 oz plain flour

2½ oz unsalted butter

1¾ oz caster sugar

A pinch of salt

1 large egg yolk

1 tablespoon of cold water

Bakewell tart:

Strawberry, raspberry or blackcurrant jam

Almond sponge or frangipane

4½ oz butter

4½ oz sugar

3 medium eggs

4½ oz ground almonds

3 oz self-raising flour

Apricot tart:

Almond sponge or frangipane

3 oz butter

3 oz sugar

2 medium eggs

3 oz ground almonds

2 oz self-raising flour

For the pastry, rub together flour and butter till it's like breadcrumbs. Then mix in sugar, a pinch of salt, a large egg yolk and a tablespoon of cold water. Gather it together in your hands and shape into a ball. If it's too dry, add a little more water. Then flatten to a disc and pop it in the fridge in a bag for 30 minutes. (Recipes always say you should use cling film, but I am sure cling film is not a healthy product and I will not use it!)

Roll it out and fold over, roll again and repeat till it's stretchy and no more than half a centimetre thick, at which point you are ready to line the tin. Cover with greaseproof paper and put the baking beans in. Pop it into the oven for about 15 minutes or till the edges start to change colour. Remove from the oven and allow to cool down.

MY LOCKDOWN COOKBOOK

For the Bakewell tart: pour a generous quantity of strawberry, raspberry or blackcurrant jam into the pastry once it is cool. Next, add the almond sponge or frangipane. Cream the butter and the sugar together, then add the eggs, then when it's a smooth mix, add the ground almonds and the self-raising flour. Mix this till smooth and pour this onto the jam.

Apricot tart

For the apricot tart: pour the frangipane onto the pastry and then gently press fresh halved apricots evenly spaced onto the frangipane. Its nice to sprinkle flaked almonds on top, too!

Put each tart in the oven at around 140°C and cook till risen and browned gently all over. For my tastes, both these need to be moist, if not gooey, in the middle, as I do not like them when they get dry. So as soon as the centre feels firm, take it out of the oven.

Allow to cool for 5–10 minutes and serve with double cream or your choice of accompaniment.

Rich Flourless Chocolate Cake

A very popular cake with chocolate lovers. Good for those intolerant to gluten. It's very rich. I adore dark chocolate so I love this. Great with fresh raspberries or blueberries on the side. Some really crazy people have cream too! Crazy, eh?

 For 12  20/25 minutes 1 hour 20/1 hour 30

35g of dark cocoa powder

1/3 cup hot water

150g dark chocolate – 70% good; 80% rich enough!

150g butter

300g dark soft sugar

125g ground almonds

4 eggs

Ganache topping:

150g dark chocolate

150 ml or 2/3 cup double cream

1 tablespoon heaped, icing sugar

Blend the cocoa with the hot water in a small bowl. Take a larger heatproof bowl and place over a saucepan with an inch or so of water in. Bring to a simmer and put the butter and chocolate in to melt. When it's all melted and mixed, take off the pan and add the cocoa mixture, sugar, ground almonds and beaten egg yolks.

Bake for 1 hour 20-25 minutes or until firm on the top. It can take a while longer as temperature is so critical as is the tin size. It won't spoil, as it's lovely when gooey.

When it's cooled, remove the sides and then mix the ganache ingredients by melting the chocolate first, then adding the cream and icing sugar together a little at a time so there are no lumps. This needs to be poured over the top. Place in a box in the fridge overnight before serving.

Rich Fruitcake – For Christmas

This very traditional cake is based upon a recipe that my mum took from her mum. I would not be surprised if it's another of those truly generational things (as I suspect the cherry cake on the next page is). We'll probably never know, sadly.

This recipe is the Xmas version of a more ordinary, less rich cake. More fruit, and alcohol feature in this version. And since I am not fond of the very sweet traditional icings, I prefer it just as it comes; you can add chopped nuts or halved almonds to the top if you like. Bake it well in advance – in the autumn!

9 oz self-raising flour

8 oz butter

7 oz soft dark sugar

3 medium eggs

2 tsp mixed cake spice

Bottle(s) of port

Bottle(s) of brandy

2½ lbs mixed cake fruit – sultanas, raisins, currants and cherries

Candied peel or walnuts (optional: neither of them work for me at all)

A couple of days before you are going to bake this, put all the fruit into a large bowl and pour in quite a lot of cheap port and cheap brandy. Turn it regularly. If the alcohol all gets sucked up, add more. Doing this over a couple of days is part of the secret to a fine, rich cake.

Cream the butter and sugar, then add the eggs one at a time, ensuring a smooth mix. Then add the flour and mixed spice and thoroughly mix it. Then add the fruit to the mix and turn into a greased lined tin.

Place in the oven at 150°C for 45 minutes and then turn down to 135°C for a further 1 hour and 15 minutes and probably more until the cake has set. Before it's taken out of the oven, the cake needs to rise in the middle and set, so you can tap the top without it wobbling. I like this cake to be moist, if not a touch gooey, but you must decide your preferred way; it may take years for you to perfect it to suit your preference!

Cool on a rack and then wrap well in foil and then seal in a plastic food bag, then place in a dark cool cupboard for at least four weeks.

Then remove the cake carefully from its wrapping, with a skewer, make many holes in the top and dribble cheap brandy or rum, which ever you prefer, in through the holes. As soon as it's sunk in, re-cover with foil and bag and store till Christmas.

I like the cake plain, but traditionally, it would be covered in marzipan and royal icing or brushed with jam and covered with toasted whole almonds. It's your choice. This cake improves with age as long as it's stored still sealed in its foil and bag and in a cool dark place.

Cherry and Almond Cake

This was made for us at home when I was a boy and then teenager. I made it for my children too, who along with their friends consumed it greedily whenever it was made.

My mum made quite a lot of cakes. No wonder I am addicted for life to cake and puddings! In those days, butter was still a luxury, so where it would not be too noticeable, most cakes were made with margarine. Clearly, shortbread did not taste good at all that way and Mum did use butter in that case. Most of the others were made with margarine. So, the day when I first made my own cherry cake, I decided then that butter was best. Wow! The taste and consistency was so much better. Since then I have made this lovely cake hundreds of times – literally. Once you have made it a few times you can experiment – blueberries or raspberries are good, but being much wetter than cherries, need longer to cook. Nothing quite matches the original for me, though.

For 10

15/20 minutes   1 hour 20/1 hour 30 minutes

8 oz butter

8 oz sugar

8 oz self-raising flour

4 medium eggs

2½ oz ground almonds (or 3 oz if you like)

¾ pot of glacé cherries, well chopped

Cream the butter and sugar till light and fluffy. Add the eggs one by one and beat well. When that's a pretty smooth liquid, add the flour and ground almonds. Stir in gently to begin with so you do not end up enveloped in a cloud! Once it's mixed in, add the cherries and complete the mix.

Spoon it in to a greased and lined cake tin and place in the fan oven at 130/140°C. This should be done in 80–90 minutes, but you need be sure the risen top is solid not wobbly, and cannot be easily pushed down.

I like it undercooked – gooey in the middle, not too dry! But it's your choice. It will not take long to know. Maybe 2–3 times to get it just the way you like it. Be precise about the temperature so you know where to set it as a few degrees either way makes a difference.

When it's cooked, take it out and put it on a board and cover with a tea towel. After letting it cool for 10–15 minutes at most, turn it out on to the board and let it cool covered. Me and my children loved this warm, but once it's cool, put it in a proper sealed tin to keep fresh.

Scones for a Cream Tea

When fresh, these are truly great, with lots of strawberry jam and Cornish clotted cream. Truly scrumptious and not at all good for anyone! There are many ways to make scones; this method is about as easy as it comes.

Many say using buttermilk is the best, so once you have perfected it with milk, try that: it is that much better and does not dry up so quickly. But, if you want a quick cream tea and do not plan to have much left over, this is as easy as it gets!

For 6–8   10 minutes   10/12 minutes

8 oz of self-raising flour
1 tsp baking powder
2 oz of butter

1 oz of sugar
A little milk

Rub the butter into the flour and baking powder till it's like coarse breadcrumbs. Stir in the sugar, then add milk to make a soft dough you can roll out. You can add a little fruit – sultanas are the usual choice.

With the dough about ½ to ¾ inch thick, cut into 2–3 inch rounds. You will need one of those plastic or metal round fluted cutters.

Take a baking tray and cover with greaseproof paper. Arrange the rounds with a little space between them. Brush with milk and bake at 220°C for about 10–12 minutes.

Let them cool properly and place them on a serving plate.

New York Cheesecake

I have always loved cheesecake: my favourite, by far, is the New York type. This I first discovered on one of many trips for work to New York. Delis served up American-size portions of this weighty, firm and very tasty cake with all sorts of extras on the side, fresh fruit and fruit sauces being the most popular. I later discovered bagel bakeries in north London that also served UK-size portions of a similar cake; theirs often had sultanas mixed in. Over the years I tried and failed many times till lockdown, when I like many had time on my hands. It took a few attempts, but this I am very pleased with.

You will need an 8-inch springform tin that's pretty deep to cook this, or just multiply all the ingredients by 50% and make a 10-inch even deeper one that's cooked longer.

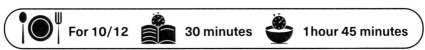

For 10/12   30 minutes   1 hour 45 minutes

For the base:

140 grams of crumbed digestive biscuits

80 grams butter

30 grams sugar

1 tsp+ cinnamon – optional

For the filling:

750 grams full fat soft cheese – Philadelphia cream cheese ideal

200 grams caster sugar

2 tbsp cornflour

2 tsp vanilla essence

3 tsp lemon juice

3 large eggs

1 large 150 ml pot of sour cream

Be sure all ingredients are at room temperature. Grease and flour the tin. Wrap the removable base in parchment paper, then re-assemble the tin and line the sides with strips of paper too. Then melt the butter in a pan and add the finely crumbled biscuits and sugar and cinnamon. Stir well so it's all mixed and turn it into the tin. Spread it evenly and pack it down firmly, then push it into the sides so it rises at least halfway up. Place in the oven at 200C for 10 minutes. Set aside.

In a mixer, put all the soft cheese in, and using the standard tool beat on slow/medium for 1 minute until it's smooth. Add in the cornflour and sugar and mix for another minute. In a medium-sized bowl, beat the eggs with the lemon juice and vanilla. With the mixer on low, add the egg mix slowly. Remove the bowl from the mixer and with a spatula fold in the sour cream. Pour into the tin on top of the baked crumb base.

Bake at 340/350°C for 1 hour 45 minutes, then turn the oven off and leave it to cool for 2 hours. Then, when it's fully cooled, take it out and put it in a cake tin/box and put it in the fridge overnight. Take it out of the fridge a couple of hours before serving. Remove the tin sides, keeping the tin base with the paper. Carefully remove the cake and place it on a plate for serving. Serve with fresh fruit, or not.

Swiss Roll

This is one of the better things for a special pudding. It really impresses when it arrives at the table! It's not that difficult at all, but most people think it's just too hard for them and they do not want to try. So read on! It's simple, really. Just a bit of handling that is soon learnt.

All you need to make this is a Swiss roll tin for the sponge to cook in, and some greaseproof paper to line the tin.

For 8   15 minutes   12 minutes + 10 minutes

4½ oz caster sugar

3 oz plain flour, sieved

3 medium eggs

½ tsp baking powder

1 tbsp cold water

200ml pot of double cream

Beat the eggs and sugar till light and fluffy. This takes time. Once it starts to lighten in colour, that's good enough.

Next, fold in the sieved flour, baking powder and water. Take the greased, lined tin and pour the mixture in and spread it more or less evenly! Bake at 200°C for 10 minutes.

Spread a sheet of greaseproof paper out and sieve more icing sugar on to it. Turn the sponge out on to this paper carefully; trim the edges if necessary. Then, while it's warm, spread with raspberry or strawberry jam so the jam melts in and allow to cool.

Take a bowl and pour in the double cream and beat it till it firms up. Once the sponge and jam has cooled, spread the cream over.

Then, using the greaseproof paper, pick up one end and roll the thing into an 'e' shape. The roll should be covered by the paper, but do not allow the paper to get inside the roll! (That's not the best description, but just check on the internet for a YouTube tutorial: once you see it, it's easy enough!)

Tuck the paper underneath so the whole roll is fixed and cannot move, then place in the fridge, covered well, to set for a few hours.

That's it! When you are ready to eat it, pick the whole thing up and place it on a serving plate and carefully remove the paper. Sieve some icing sugar onto the roll before taking to the table.

Looks pretty. Tastes great, too.

Victoria Sponge

A classic English cake. Like the Swiss roll, it's actually easy to make. You can fill with just jam, jam and fresh cream, jam and buttercream... Many variations.

This recipe is just for the sponge. You can make the whole thing in one tin – the sort with a removable base. When it's cooked and cooled down, you just need a long sharp knife to slice it in half and a clean hand to put it on a board and a little later place it on top.

 For 8–10   25/30 minutes   40/45 minutes

6 oz butter

6 oz self-raising flour

6 oz caster sugar

3 good size eggs

About half a dozen drops vanilla essence

Cream the butter and sugar till it's changing colour. Add the eggs one at a time and beat well to a smooth mix, fold in the sieved flour and add the vanilla. The lighter this mix is, the fluffier and lighter the sponge.

Take an 8-inch tin with removable base, grease it and flour it, then pour in the mix. Place in the oven at about 150°C until it's nicely risen and the top is browned, about 40–45 minutes. Let it cool on a wire rack. Then slice it in two and fill with your choice.

My preference is a very generous spreading of strawberry jam, and a well sprinkled icing sugar top! No rules. My mum used the same generous jam and then beaten smooth buttercream with more vanilla. It's also nice with raspberry jam and fresh cream. Classic cake for tea. Enjoy.

My Christmas Pudding

This is one of the very special things for me every Christmas. I love the richness and fruity flavours which, when mixed with brandy butter, cream or custard, is a treat in a bowl, every day till it's gone! Mum made her own every year when I was home, as she did with Christmas cake and mince pies.

So this is a family recipe, only with annual improvements. Every year, I have adjusted or even left out items in order to improve it, to make it vegetarian, and to improve the flavour. It's pretty good now: almost perfect. But next year I will try a little change.

This recipe makes enough to fill a 7-inch glass/Pyrex bowl, which can be pressure-cooked, steamed or microwaved.

4 oz vegetarian suet

Grated zest of 1 large orange

4 oz of mixed flour

Grated zest of 1 large lemon

2.5 oz ground almonds

2 large eggs

2 tsp mixed spice

150–200 ml Guinness

½ tsp nutmeg

1 large apple cored, peeled and chopped

½ tsp cinnamon

8 oz soft dark sugar

8 oz sultanas

8 oz raisins

10 oz currants

Quite simply, just take a big mixing bowl and chuck it all in, and half the Guinness. Mix for a good 8–10 minutes and you will have a thick, gooey mix. Then, slowly add more Guinness till it's really quite sloppy. It's not an exact science: the thing to be sure of is, it's not too thick and it's well mixed.

Now, grease and flour all the inside of your bowl, then pour in the mix. Cover the top with greaseproof paper and then a layer of foil.

The tricky bit is folding it over, and making a handle of medium string to lift the whole thing in and out of your cooking pot. If you have a bowl with a thick lip it's much easier, but you need to pass the string underneath and over a few times, crossing over in the middle, so that looking at your bowl from above you have string every 90 degrees and a way of lifting it all. It takes practice, but once you have made it every year, it gets easy – just another process.

I put mine in a pressure cooker for two and a half hours. Then on Xmas day, a few hours before we want the pudding, we give it another hour in the pressure cooker. You can steam it instead: 2½ hours in a pressure cooker = 8 hours steaming, roughly!

After Boxing Day, I simply warm a portion in a small bowl, as I am the only one who continues to greedily eat it. That's 30–45 seconds in a microwave!

CAKES AND PUDDINGS

Carrot Cake

At last, after so many different recipes for carrot cake, none of which suited my tastes or desires, this recipe is it!! It's just how I think carrot cake should be.

I've never liked the oil that most recipes call for, and quite frankly the nuts are not relevant in my world either. I love nuts of many sorts – my favourite is probably home-roasted cashews with a little chilli and honey – but not in cake.

280g self-raising flour

330g soft dark sugar

180g butter

3 medium eggs

150g sultanas

330g organic carrots, grated

juice of one large orange

1½ tsp cinnamon

1½ tsp nutmeg

1½ tsp ginger

½ tsp salt

Cream the butter and sugar, then add the eggs and mix thoroughly, then the flour, spices and salt. Next the orange juice, the sultanas and finally the peeled and grated carrots. This should give a very moist and quite sloppy mix. Grease a bread tin (or 20cm round) and line with parchment paper. Spoon the mix in and place in the middle of the fan oven at 140°C for 1 hour 30 minutes, or until the cake has risen and not wobbly.

For the topping:

200g cream cheese

110g butter

175g icing sugar

1 tsp vanilla essence

Mix the topping ingredients together until smooth.

Let the cake cool, carefully remove the paper and then spread the topping evenly over the top of the cake. Place it somewhere cool for a couple of hours to allow topping to set and then its ready to serve. Keep in an airtight box, but not in the fridge unless it's a heatwave.

I could eat a lot of this.

Try it yourself. It's easy.

Summer Pudding

For 10–12   45 minutes   overnight in fridge

This was a pudding I would order in a restaurant. I love puddings and fruit – for me, cake, tart and pudding, all a must. Learning to make them myself was a challenge I happily took on. Buying the fruit in mixed bags from a supermarket freezer is just as good as spending twice as much on fresh fruit ,which is rarely available all at the same time. To my memory, all major family and friend gatherings included this pudding and there was never a morsel left. Shame!

So, you need a good size bowl, and a saucer that, upside down, just fits inside the top! A loaf of medium sliced white bread, a couple of lemons and some sugar, plus the bags of fruit – summer fruit.

Tip two bags of frozen mixed fruit into a good sized saucepan. Let it defrost, turn the cooker to low heat and slowly warm the fruit. It will bubble and give off some juice. This takes time; do not let it get hot. Stir regularly. When it's well warmed, just hot enough not to want to touch, add a cup of sugar and some pectin. Pectin is a substance used to 'set' jam; it helps the fruit to 'firm up', so when the pudding is served it keeps its shape. If pectin is not available, add the juice of one and a half lemons. This should do the job. You will need to keep going for 10 more minutes. Stir occasionally to be sure it's truly mixed in.

Open the medium sliced white loaf – yes, against my principles I know, but it's the way this works best. Grease and flour the bowl. Then, cut all the crusts off and line the entire bowl with the slices, cutting to fit and being sure to leave no gaps. Pour the well-warmed fruit and all the juice into the bowl. Make a lid with the remainder of the bread – again, leaving no gaps. Finally, place the saucer upside down on top so that it fits inside the bowl and is pressing the whole lot down. Place a large-size, heavy tin of beans or similar on top as a weight, and just push it gently to force juice into all the bread, then put it in the fridge overnight.

The next day, remove the tin and the saucer, turn the pudding upside down onto a serving plate with sides that turn up, to catch any juice, and let the whole thing slowly drop safely onto the plate. If it does not, shout a bit, then try to get a thin, bendy spatula around the sides and try again. If it still will not shift, curse a bit, give up, and serve from the bowl. I have only once suffered this indignity. It still tasted lovely and was all eaten; it just did not look quite so impressive. Best served with double cream.

Strawberry and Cream Cake

I was treated to this at a summer fair, made and donated by a very good baker indeed. So I had no idea what was in it, or anything really. I did know it tasted great and being the cake fiend that I am, I had to try to work it out. This recipe is the result of all that 'research'!

For 8–10

20/30 minutes   1 hour 15/1 hour 20 minutes

120g self-raising flour

140g ground almonds

250g butter

250g caster sugar

zest of a lemon

4 good size eggs

1 tsp at least of vanilla essence

200g or firm sweet strawberries

Medium size pot of double cream

So, cream the butter and sugar. Add the eggs and beat well till it's all well mixed and full of bubbles. Gently fold in the flour and the ground almonds along with the vanilla and the zest of lemon. Try to keep some bubbles intact

Pour into a greased and lined 8-inch round tin with a removable base that's about 4–5 cm deep. Pop in the oven at about 150°C for at least 75 minutes.

The way you will know it's done is by the top! Give it a tap with a finger and if it wobbles it's not done: you do not want this cake to be gooey in the middle. It needs to be like a Victoria sponge – risen and evenly cooked, with a brown crisped top and almost fluffy inside.

Once this is cooked, remove from the oven, remove from the tin and place on a wire rack to cool down.

Once it's cooled down, remove the paper and slice through the middle. Place the bottom half on a board or plate, thinly slice some of the strawberries to cover it and then spoon some whipped cream on top, evenly spread. Place the other half on top, then cover the top with double cream, well-beaten so it's firm. Cover that with chopped strawberries.

Truly delicious, and just the same as the cake I was given to try. If you want to add a little extra, I now spread strawberry jam thinly across both halves before the fruit and cream go on. It's a small thing but does add something!

Tips and Advice

Cooking takes practice. If you live to eat rather than eat to live, you will enjoy cooking. Do not be afraid of experimenting. Nothing is that difficult unless of course you follow a traditional French recipe, which I could never have the patience to do. That's why good restaurants exist!

You can make a soufflé or Swiss roll if I can: it's nothing to be scared of, really, and once you have succeeded with the soufflé recipe a couple of times, try adding some flaked salmon, or if you feel flush, some white crab meat. You know what you like and what things you like to combine, so have a go. Chunks of meat or anything heavy in a soufflé will just sink to the bottom; other than that, go for it!

Cooking times make all the difference, as do levels of heat. Casseroles generally are better the longer you cook and on a lower heat, especially beef, pork and lamb. If you cook a steak or a piece of fish, many people would say you cannot undercook it, only ruin it by cooking too long (shellfish excluded, of course). There are not many things for me that are better than fresh tuna steak, coated in freshly ground pepper and seared on the outside in a very hot smoky pan that's served so it's still largely uncooked but not cold on the inside. I feel the same about a good steak too: a hot pan with a little oil, seared on both sides.

Vegetables are the same. When I was a child, all vegetables were cooked to the point where there was no resistance whatsoever to a knife or fork, so I was not so keen. Since I learnt to cook, many people have said my veg is not cooked enough: too crisp. Well, I get that and am still trying to get the right balance.

Fresh broccoli from Tesco will take 5–7 minutes to cook so the stalks are edible, yet the same type of broccoli from a farm shop that was harvested the previous day only needs 3–5 minutes. So getting things just right can be difficult. How many TV shows about great restaurants have we watched where the head chef repeats over and over the need for supplies to be delivered to the same degree of freshness – whether it's the age of the steak, or how long ago the broccoli was picked and how long it had been grown for, and so on?

Cooking is not a science, although an understanding of science will help: if anything, it's an art. So be prepared to make a judgement on what you cook, and adjust each time until it's as good as it can be, in your judgement! For me, the obsession with presentation is all very well if you want to run a posh restaurant, but good food is more about how it tastes than how it looks.

Marinades

It's very easy to make these using a plastic bag. You can massage the contents. It is not that different from putting it all in a bowl and giving it a regular stir, I just find it better and easier and it's more of a guarantee that all the meat or fish will get covered, and you do not need as much either. I just wish there was such a thing as environmentally friendly plastic that's readily available and actually works. Soon, maybe.

For all meat and fish, you can invent marinades for yourselves! The way marinades work is quite simple, really. Think of a Mexican ceviche, mostly lime juice, and that's because it tenderises all meats and fish. So lime is a great ingredient for a marinade. Lemon is okay too, but not so strong. Honey is another ingredient that helps those BBQs blacken around the edges, and it does the same in a hot oven. So if you go to the Chipotle Pork Chop recipe that I slowly perfected, it's lime and honey added to the Chipotle sauce and grilled. Works so well.

Try your favourite flavours with the basic ingredients. For summer BBQs, my basic marinade (in a bag again) is very simple. For lamb, it's olive oil, lime juice and garlic with fresh rosemary. Chicken is either the tikka paste from the recipe in this book, or again, olive oil, garlic and lime juice with some fresh herb from the garden, like oregano. A home-made BBQ sauce is great, too: you can make it in batches like curry pastes. Garlic, ginger, onion, chilli, ketchup, soy, lime or lemon, Lea & Perrins, and so many more ingredients – depending on what you like.

Cut portions of meat and fish and put them in a bag with some home-made BBQ sauce and get the BBQ hot. Skewer the pieces or just place on the griddle, brush more marinade on to keep it moist and be sure it's cooked through – except, of course, beef or lamb, which I always like a little pink.

Rice

It's easy to go along with the old and trusted way to boil rice in a big pot of water and strain, but this is my 100% method that's easier and I think better. Wash the rice thoroughly first. Then take the following guidelines to measure:

- Thai sticky rice – 1 cup of rice to ⅞ cup water, for 10 minutes
- Thai fragrant rice – 1 cup of rice to 1⅛ cups of water, for 10 minutes
- Japanese rice – 1 cup of rice to 1¼ cups of water for 10 minutes
- Basmati rice – 1 cup rice to 1½ cups of water for 10 minutes
- Whole grain basmati – 1 cup of rice to 1¾ cups of water for 16 minutes
- Red rice – 1 cup of rice to 1¾ cups of water for 18 minutes

So, bring these to the boil fully, then place a well-fitting lid on, turn down to a minimum and simmer using a timer for the set time. When the timer pings, do not take the lid off: just leave for 5 minutes in the case of the 10-minute rice or 8–10 minutes for the longer. Then it's ready, the water is absorbed and it's ready to eat from the pot.

If you like fried rice, it's easy with brown rice saved in the freezer or cooked earlier. White rice sticks too easily. Always fry the other ingredients first and then add the brown rice and stir till it's steamy hot. Often it needs a splash of water or soy or some other flavoured liquid you may want to try. Be brave: it will not be a disaster, but you may find a version that suits your taste buds.

All rice except sticky rice and Japanese rice freezes very well, despite the health warnings online. I have been doing this for many years. The practice should be to put it in a pot, well pressed down, as soon as it's cool, and with a good fitting lid. However, if you have not eaten it within a month, remove from the freezer and bin it!

Taste

Many moons ago I filmed a long sequence of the scientist Robert Winston presenting *Child of Our Time* for the BBC, all about this subject. He said to camera that we fall into five main categories, and this explains why some people love Marmite and others (like me) loathe it. So, my only reason for this is to say, what I like may not suit you! You may like it sweeter, or saltier, or more vinegary, and so on. Do not be shy of experimenting or adjusting to your taste. It's the same with chilli or garlic and other spices: try adjusting if you feel you need to. I am not wrong and neither are you; we just have different perceptions of flavour. These might be quite small differences but they can decide whether a dish is five-star or four-, and that can be quite a big thing for us foodie folks.

Stock

Here is a big subject. Read a Larousse cookbook, France's finest, and they would have you believe a proper stock takes days and has many, many ingredients.

This is what I believe – chicken stock works for everything, unless you are a veggie.

After your Sunday roast chicken, pop all the bones, minus the skin, into a big pot. Chuck in a bit of carrot, a medium onion and any discarded vegetable peelings, plus generous salt and pepper. Boil, then simmer with the lid on for a couple of hours. Strain it and save in small portions to put in the freezer.

If you want to make stock for Eastern food, it's the same, but chuck in a star anise or two, a couple of cloves and a chunk of ginger, roughly chopped. For veggie stock: carrot, onion, leek and more, gently fried in oil, then add water and seasoning and simmer for an hour or so.

MY LOCKDOWN COOKBOOK

I have not had any issues with these versions of stock. They are quick and easy. They work with anything from risotto to Tom Yam soup. It's not fine cuisine, it's home cooking.

Oils

For health reasons I believe we should only use pressed oils like olive, peanut or sesame oils. Not the industrially processed oils. Coconut oil is a good replacement for ghee in curries. Very expensive oils are better for a treat on a salad or similar, but never waste them on a cooked dish. Duck fat makes just the best roast or sautéed potatoes.

Ingredients

Herbs make a huge difference to many recipes, and those who can grow pots on a window sill or a garden will truly notice the fragrance and flavour of freshly grown herbs. Home-grown tomatoes with fresh basil are both bursting with flavour and a joy. A pot of fast-growing garlic chives add that little extra to European as well as East Asian dishes, and do not be misled: coriander or sweet Thai basil can easily be grown here too. In my kitchen garden, I have mint, thyme, parsley, chives, basil, oregano, marjoram, sage and rosemary, with a plan to add more in the spring. It's really worth the small effort.

For all Asian dishes, the same advice applies: do not bother with dried lemongrass or a jar of crushed garlic, unless you really need to save time. They are a let-down compared to the fresh versions from the local store. Asian stores the length and breadth of the UK now stock lemongrass and turmeric, for example, along with the now ubiquitous ginger and chillies, and much more. You may think you need to save time, but honestly, with a little practice, the difference is negligible in time but considerable in taste! Your choice, of course; just beware of some prepared stuff that contains e-numbers. I try to avoid these mostly, but check the web and see what they are, as some are truly innocuous.

Never buy cheap soy! The Chinese ones can contain some pretty bad stuff, so do your health a favour and buy a big bottle of Kikkoman or a similar Japanese one. Beware when buying all sorts of East Asian preparations: some are to be avoided, and you can find out online quite easily which brands to avoid.

Sambal Olek is a very useful thing to have around and I rely on it quite a lot. On the bottle it should be basically chopped chillies and oil, with other recognisable things. I find Waitrose's own quite good; maybe a little more expensive, but not enough to worry about. Shopping at Wing Yip on London's North Circular was a great adventure, but since the beginning of lockdown I have only been there online. It's fine if you know what you want; delivery is slow, however. You can see all the ingredients of each sauce and check health sites, etc., for safety and efficacy.

When it comes to the more ordinary stuff like potatoes or tomatoes, again, be aware that there are many differing flavours and uses. Red potatoes can be a lovely thing baked in the oven, but compared to the King Edward, an English staple, they need at least 15–20 minutes more cooking time and are tastier. The small Charlotte potatoes, for example, are lovely boiled with a quiche and smothered with melted butter or made into a salad with chives, mint and mayo. Onions, too: red onions are great in salads and chutneys, shallots are really for Asian cooking and casseroles, whilst the trusty big white ones should be used in a chilli con carne where their robustness and size are perfect.

By and large, farm shops are the place to buy fresh produce if you are country folks, but if not, make a list and go and support your local fruit and veg shop. The produce may be a bit muddy, but so fresh – so much so that purple broccoli in my local is completely different from what is found on the shelf for twice the price in Tesco. The pak choi bought there is smaller, crispier and much tastier than the fat, overgrown supermarket stuff.

Presentation and Combination

Many curries have similar ingredients such as turmeric, coriander and cumin, which can often make these dishes an orange through to a brown colour. The reason commercial chicken tikka is usually red is that they add a colouring to enhance the look of the dish. I would never advise that!

Beef in any part of the world cooked slowly will end up dark brown. Tomatoes in a sauce end up red. Salad and veg tend to be more green. Does presentation actually matter at all? Well, it does. A plate of sloppy, orangey-brown glop is never going to be mouth-watering. But if you have already had this glop and it's an amazing treat, then it will be mouth-watering. So, taste is all, really – almost – though a little thought on presentation goes a long way. Improve the look of sauces with a dressing of chopped herbs or finely sliced chillies. Score the surface of a steak or a chop before cooking to add interest. Add some chopped chives or a teaspoon of Dijon mustard to mash. Mix up colours and textures in a salad. In general, just as you might consider how to combine flavours, and which dishes work with others, so too with colours. It's not a big deal. If you are serving two veg with a meal, make them different in texture, colour and taste, if you can. It is psychological, like so many things in life.

A little care when it comes to presentation, even at home, just makes you feel you are eating something a bit special. So get the pretty serving bowls out!

Choose ovenware that comes to the table and does not look out of place. Get a few big serving plates for your roasted joint or your Swiss roll.

As for flavours that work together, duck and pork are considered quite fatty meats, so they are often served with robustly flavoured veg like braised red cabbage or cavolo nero. The boldly flavoured chipotle pork chop (page 108) works very well with coleslaw and a tomato and onion salad, and presents well too. A quiche – essentially eggs and cheese – has quite a gentle flavour, so boiled new potatoes, with mint or chives and melted butter, work well with a veg or salad on the side. For me, I can eat fish and rice or chicken and rice, served with salad or veg, every day. Lots of different sorts of rice, endless varieties of fish, and endless ways to cook chicken. Great combinations! Healthy, quick and tasty. My wife would agree, but would always swap the rice for potatoes.

I love curries and tagines. They say variety is the spice of life; I so agree. Tagines and some curries manage to combine spices, meat, and fruit all together, which is quite something. My Pork and Prunes (page 112) is a dish from nearer to home. So it's possible, with imagination, to mix all sorts of things together. So many cuisines with such great flavour and taste to explore. Be bold. Do not be nervous or put off.

Implements

We are fortunate, too, today, in that the tools that help with everyday cooking are not expensive and are easy to buy online. If you like curries and East Asian foods, a spice grinder and a pestle and mortar will be really helpful, and they are not at all expensive. A food processor will chop, blend, mix, and knead.

Avoid the cheapest pots and pans: in the long run you will have to replace them regularly, as the non-stick surfaces crumble away, or the thin bottom of pots and pans warp and burn and the handles will fall off too. Le Creuset stuff is brilliant, but the prices are crazy, and similar cast iron casseroles and pans will be far less than half the price. A Pyrex casserole dish with a lid will do, as you can start your dish in a pan on the hob.

Go to a ProCook store for good equipment at fair prices. Good sharp knives are a must, but you can buy a sharpener for just a few pounds and sharpening your knives is so quick and easy. You cannot cook with pastry without a rolling pin, but a wooden one is less than £10. You will need a few wooden spoons for stirring. A couple of good spatulas will be useful for sauces and removing the contents of your pans into serving bowls.

MY LOCKDOWN COOKBOOK

Buy baking trays in multiples, as they are cheap and often used. Earthenware dishes are ideal for roasting chicken joints and sausages, perfect for cauliflower cheese too.

You will need some bowls of differing sizes – I prefer the Pyrex glass type, but that's just me – for beating eggs and whipping cream.

These are the basic kitchen tools I have. Plus a selection of pots and pans, from a small non-stick saucepan to a large 26cm stainless steel saucepan and a similar range of frying pans. Then a few oven-safe dishes of differing size. Make a collection as and when you can. Then bowls: start with a few plastic ones if you need to, then acquire glass ovenproof ones as and when. As for knives, in the beginning I relied upon a few Victorinox knives – plastic-handled, very sharp – that were exceptionally cheap, then I slowly acquired stronger ones that I could sharpen easily myself. Depending upon space of course, a selection of different sizes and shapes of serving plates and bowls is useful.

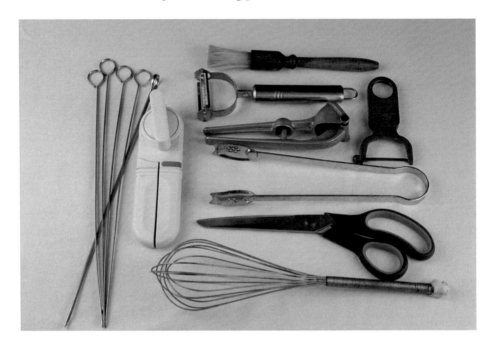

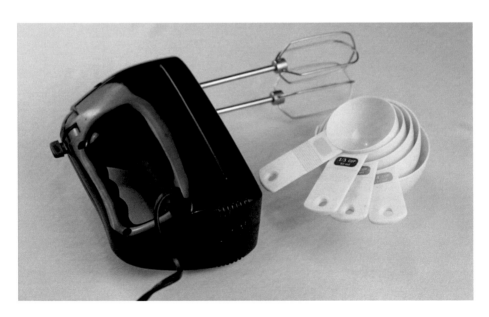

MY LOCKDOWN COOKBOOK

We Survived the Pandemic!

Well, only just!

Many of us will have the mental scars for a very long while.

Many of us will miss those that fell.

All of us will never forget.

Things can only get better – we hope.

Deserted beaches, parks and mothballed pubs, TV news and the papers full of eerie shots of central London looking like we had not survived! We all imagined we were in fact living through a Hollywood disaster movie. Socially distanced queues at supermarkets and empty shelves, loo roll and flour out of stock for weeks. No football and no cricket! For the first time since the war, many of our cultural pleasures were being denied.

Here in our country home, gardening and cooking became a way of life; reading and learning, too. We had to gain something, despite the terrible losses. There was a certain joy from learning, albeit slowly, how to raise crops. It was almost shocking that a fresh homegrown potato could taste so good. Tomatoes that were so sweet and crisp they really could rightly be called fruit. Courgettes, beans and peas, purple 'heritage' carrots, all brought a big smile. Salad leaves that seemed to grow so fast you could almost watch them grow; these salads had a vibrant crunch not known before. Then, too much! A big harvest. Time to make chutneys, spicy ketchup and other preserves. Apple and plum crumble. Strawberry tart.

High summer was hot summer. The joy of picking, cutting and digging up so many foods: it may be a steep learning curve for me, but it's also a huge surprise to taste fruit and veg that has had no chemicals to help it grow. Yes, the insects and birds had their share, and more at times, but we still had plenty.

So after years of living in London and travelling widely, living in the countryside has opened up new ways to live, to eat and to grow. The environment really does matter, and what we eat is part of that. The wildlife here is still diverse and abundant and we share our space with it, willingly.

This world of ours in the only one we have. The likes of Jeff Bezos, Elon Musk and Richard Branson have come under fire for beginning to look elsewhere for resources in the short term and places to live too. But we need these explorers.

MY LOCKDOWN COOKBOOK